Other Resources from David and Claudia Arp:

Books
Answering the 8 Cries of the Spirited Child
10 Great Dates Before You Say "I Do"
10 Great Dates to Energize Your Marriage
Love Life for Parents
The Second Half of Marriage
Empty Nesting
Suddenly They're 13!
Quiet Whispers from God's Heart for Couples
52 Dates for You and Your Mate
Marriage Moments
Family Moments

Video Curriculum
10 Great Dates to Energize Your Marriage
The Second Half of Marriage
PEP Groups for Parents

FOCUS ON THE FAMILY®

Loving Your Relatives

David & Claudia Arp and John & Margaret Bell

TYNDALE

Tyndale House Publishers, Wheaton, Illinois

To the memory of those family members who have gone before us,
in appreciation for the steadfast love of those who are with us,
and in hope for those who follow us, we dedicate this book.

Contents

Acknowledgments

We are deeply indebted to the many people who contributed to this project and gratefully acknowledge the contributions of the following:

The hundreds of people who took time to respond to our survey with their suggestions, thoughts, and concerns about being family.

All the many couples who have participated in our Marriage Alive seminars over the years and have shared with us their struggles and success stories dealing with extended family.

Those who have pioneered family and marriage education and on whose shoulders we stand, including James Dobson, David and Vera Mace, Gary Smalley, John Trent, Les and Leslie Parrott, Mike and Harriet McManus, David and Jan Stoop, Sharon Hart Morris, Norm Wright, Dennis and Emily Lowe, and Scott Stanley. We especially thank Diane Sollee for all she has done and is doing to encourage family and marriage education.

Our Focus on the Family team who have believed in and supported us in this project, for your encouragement and excitement about this new resource. We especially thank Mark Maddox, Tom Spitza, Julie Kuss, and our editor, Larry Weeden, and his in-house team. You are fantastic and fun to work with! Thanks also go to Jane Terry, Susan Graham, Ken Roth, and all the great Focus Over Fifty team who encouraged us along the way.

Michele Bartlett, who provided excellent editing just when we needed it the most.

Laurie Clark and John and Jane Bell, who offered insightful suggestions.

Our literary agent, Greg Johnson of Alive Communications, for being our advocate and encouraging us along the way.

Foreword

The late, brilliant thinker Francis Schaeffer used to say that the greatest challenge for Christians is to exhibit the love of God and the holiness of God at the same time. Or, as one of our favorite preachers Dr. Stuart Briscoe once said, "Christians are to be both sweet and strong." While these men were talking in general about all of life, we can also think of no better counsel with regard to maintaining healthy family relationships.

I (Tullian) was blessed to grow up in a solid Christian home. The middle of seven children (four brothers and two sisters), I saw authentic faith lived out before my eyes. My dad, a well-known and respected psychologist, has always put his family before anybody or anything. My mom, the eldest daughter of Billy and Ruth Graham, is an award-winning author and speaker whose commitment to discipling her children surpassed any other ambition. Yet, while my brothers and sisters rarely gave my parents any real trouble, I was a different story!

For various reasons (some of which are presented in Challenge 6 of this book), my parents had to kick me (Tullian) out of the house when I was 16 years old. Because my destructive lifestyle was so harmful to the rest of the family, my parents had to exercise tremendous "strength," to exhibit the "holiness of God" and flex their parental muscles. They did not do this, however, with an absence of love. In fact, the love of God compelled them to action. They loved me, and the rest of the family, too much to let the destruction continue. Their strength was sweet and their sweetness was strong.

I did not come back to the Lord until I was 21 years old. But during those "wilderness years," my parents maintained this simultaneous exhibition of God's love and God's holiness, of sweetness and strength. They never allowed me to move back into the house because of the way I was choosing to live (strength), but they never shut me out of the family (sweetness).

Schaeffer went on to say that when we show either God's love or God's holiness without the other, we exhibit "not the character of God, but a caricature of God." My parents' accurate exhibition of the character of God is the tool God used to bring me back, not only to Himself, but also into a healthy relationship with them and the rest of my family.

Dave and Claudia Arp, along with John and Margaret Bell, have provided a practical blueprint for those of us who are trying to exhibit the love of God and the holiness of God at the same time within our families. They show how we can, and should, be both sweet and strong as we deal with our immediate and extended families. They recognize rightly that life in the family is not always easy, that there are crooked branches in every family tree, whether they be in the form of persons or circumstances. They have captured the truth that God designed family life, not simply for our *happiness*, but more importantly for our *holiness*. And with that in mind, the Arps and the Bells show throughout this book that family life can and should be satisfying.

Thank you, Dave and Claudia, John and Margaret, for this practical guide that will, we're sure, prove to be of tremendous help to all who read it.

—W. TULLIAN TCHIVIDJIAN AND GIGI GRAHAM TCHIVIDJIAN

Part One

The Extended Family of the Twenty~First Century

Welcome to the Extended Family

Everyone is part of an extended family, and most everyone will readily admit to some tension somewhere in their extended-family tree. One reason might be that you can choose your mate, but you can't choose your relatives. You can't choose your parents, your siblings, or whom they decide to marry. When we write about the extended family, we're thinking of parents, grandparents, offspring, siblings, in-laws, aunts, uncles, cousins, nieces, nephews, and even step- and adopted relatives.

For most of us, our extended family is a mixed bag. Some relatives you adore and make great pains to connect with, while others may give you such great pains you avoid them. But deep down most of us would admit that our heart's desire is really to "be family"—to belong to, connect with, enjoy, and be comfortable with our relatives. And that's what this book is all about.

We know extended family issues can be tough, so we want to give you practical helps and hope that things can get better—can actually be great! We've done our homework and have surveyed hundreds of family members around the country. When we asked, "What are your major concerns that you would like to see addressed in a book?" one participant wrote: "I need some effective tools for relating to my extended family. I'm looking for something beyond the 'suck it up' or 'you really don't need to do that' advice. In other words, how do you lovingly confront in-laws and even your own parents? How can you foster better understanding between the generations and build healthy relationships even in the midst of different views and perspectives? Please tell me. I need help and I'm all ears!"

This is precisely why we wrote this book, and in what follows we want to give you the necessary tools for understanding and relating to your extended family. But first let us introduce you to the Scott family.

MEET THE SCOTTS

Use your imagination or maybe your memory. Try to visualize that exciting, anticipated, yet often dreaded Wednesday before Thanksgiving when people across America embark on an annual pilgrimage toward some sort of family gathering to celebrate this major holiday. Many Americans have in mind a "Norman Rockwell Thanksgiving," but the reality is generally far different from that in the mind's eye.

Perhaps your experience is not so unlike the Scott family's ...

Say Hello to Paul and Gloria Scott

Paul and Gloria Scott are the parents of four grown children, grandparents of five, and soon-to-be stepgrandparents of two. Paul and Gloria are retired and have recently downsized to a condominium in a gated community. Today they are busy preparing for the arrival of their extended family for Thanksgiving.

Paul has quit fiddling with his new digital camera that he got last Christmas from his eldest son but has never used. He decides to let one of the children figure out how to make the blasted thing work, so he can e-mail this year's Christmas card picture that he is sure to get this weekend. He has just made his umpteenth trip to the grocery store for Gloria while she double-checks her list—her eldest son's favorite chai tea has been purchased, plenty of snacks are on hand for her son-in-law, Steve, who has such an appetite! In addition, she had the piano tuned for Sean; bought puzzles, videos, and comic books for the grandchildren; and made Hayley's favorite green bean casserole, dinner rolls, and pies for Thanksgiving dinner.

Paul and Gloria have worked hard to make things perfect. They are already exhausted but very excited and—truthfully—a little anxious: They don't want a repeat of their summer vacation when everybody got mad (for reasons no one can now remember) and some family members left early. Mainly, they pray that this year everyone will experience a happy and harmonious extended family Thanksgiving—just like the Thanksgivings Gloria remembers from her childhood.

Meet J. Paul Jr., the Firstborn
Their firstborn child, J. Paul Scott Jr., and his wife, Julia, pull out of their downtown loft in their Range Rover with their two children, Trey (14) and Kaitlin (7). It is only a 45-minute drive to his parents' house in the suburbs, but they still tote along a gourmet picnic purchased at a local upscale deli.

J. Paul Jr. is talking animatedly on his hands-free cell phone to his stockbroker while trying to program the GPS system—his new electronic toy. Julia is still upset that they aren't going to her mother's for the holidays. Also, her nerves are frazzled because she is responsible for the annual zoo charity benefit next week, so she covers her ears with her new Bose headphones and listens to relaxing waterfall sounds.

Meanwhile, Kaitlin pretends to watch a DVD—*The Parent Trap*—but silently pouts about leaving her new hamster for the weekend. Finally, Trey focuses more intently on his Game Boy, refusing to watch the aforementioned "chick flick."

J. Paul Jr. is thinking about what a waste of his time this is. He had tickets to the hockey game but had to pass. Julia is hoping that Hayley's (J. Paul Jr.'s youngest sister) plane is delayed or that she gets sick. Kaitlin is already complaining about Grandmother's food. And Trey is wondering if he will be pestered by his younger cousins.

Meet Jan, the Second Child
Meanwhile, J. Paul Jr.'s younger sister, Jan, and her husband, Steve, have begun their journey in their eight-year-old minivan with 165,000 miles and bald tires with their three children, Derek (9), Sally (8), and Robert (4); their yellow Labrador retriever; and a cooler with ham sandwiches, apples, chips, carrot sticks, and Oreos.

Steve is singing along to his favorite country/western station. Jan is flipping absentmindedly through the *Ladies' Home Journal*. Derek and Sally are playing Auto Bingo, and Robert is trying to manage his Bob the Builder coloring book and the box of Crayolas in his lap without the crayons rolling everywhere.

They haven't had any time to think about how things will be at Grandmother's condo. Steve is fretting about his Sunday school lesson; Jan is wondering if she remembered to feed the fish.

Meet Sean, the Third Child

Sean, the third child and a free spirit, is hurtling down the highway in his new BMW convertible with his friend Rafael, whom he met while backpacking in the Himalayas. They are listening to *Madam Butterfly* at a hundred decibels. The convertible top is down with the heater turned to MAX for the most advantageous and highly desirable tanning situation. The sporadic conversation is firmly centered on where the best gym to work out may be found, which of the boxes of exquisite chocolates from their recent trip to Belgium should be opened first, and whether the new gourmet coffee roaster/grinder/vacuum brewer they brought can handle the amount of beans necessary if everyone wants coffee.

Sean is excited about seeing all of his relatives even though he thinks they are all kind of old-fashioned. But he is really looking forward to going out on the town with Rafael to see his old high school pals after everybody else goes to bed. He also wonders if his parents can spot him some money until his new business starts to turn a profit.

Meet Hayley, the Youngest

Hayley, the baby of the family and still in graduate school, is at the airport with her former professor and now fiancé, Bill. They are joined by his two children from his first marriage, Jennifer and Willie. Hayley is prattling on and on about how much she is looking forward to sleeping in, being waited on, and eating her mother's fabulous cooking—although she hopes her mother doesn't serve that ghastly green bean casserole.

Jennifer, age 12, is busy feigning indifference while she listens to Britney Spears on her personal CD player and making mental notes to share with her mother when this whole tragically awful weekend is over. Willie, age 10, has wangled 10 dollars from his dad to disappear into the airport video arcade while they wait to board.

Bill regrets not bringing his laptop as a carry-on so he could work on the book he is writing. Hayley is thinking only of herself and wondering how her parents will react to their future stepgrandchildren.

This imminent extended family Thanksgiving could be the setting for a movie, but we all wonder, will it be a comedy, tragedy, drama, or love story?

WELCOME TO THE EXTENDED FAMILY!

Do you identify with any members of the Scott family? If we're honest, no one has a perfect family—or extended family. Within every extended family exists potential for misunderstandings, hurt feelings, anger, jealousy, fear, and anxiety. But the potential also exists for true communication, mutual understanding, healthy humor, joy, and love.

In the following pages we hope to help you understand the dynamics at work in your extended family and—with God's help—assist you in making your extended family as harmonious, healthy, and happy as it can possibly be. We will consider some of the family dynamics that affect intergenerational relationships.

When children marry, have children of their own, or perhaps inherit stepchildren, family life gets complicated. Romantic visions are often quickly shattered, and it seems that none of us lives happily ever after: The devastation of divorce, the complications of remarriage, blended families, cohabitation, or choosing an alternative lifestyle distort the Norman Rockwell image of the happy family. Families that were close growing up may find that just because their nuclear family worked doesn't mean their extended family will. Further complicating the extended family, relatives often live all over the world in this modern age.

In the midst of such complexity, how can we develop our family relationships in ways that build each other up and glorify God? We encourage you to read on.

Wherever you are in your extended family constellation, we invite you to join us as we explore that society called family.

Meet Your Guides

Because this is a book about the whole family in all seasons of life, we want to introduce you to your extended family guides. We (Dave and Claudia

Arp) are the seasoned guides. We are parents and grandparents and have been growing our own family tree for many years. We're here to give you insights in relating to your parents and grandparents and in-laws. And for those who are in our season of family life, we want to guide you in how to build better relationships with your adult children and grandchildren.

For the past 25 years we have worked as marriage and family educators, leading seminars across the United States and in Europe. We've also developed several marriage and parenting programs used by churches and community groups. We have three adult sons and eight grandchildren and have logged 40 years in our own marriage. We've been around the block a time or two and have what we hope is some sage advice to pass along. We'll be focusing on those of us who are in the second half of family life.

We (John and Margaret Bell) will speak for middle and younger generations. We have been married for 20 years and have two active teenage daughters, 14 and 17. We are in the very middle of our family tree: We are parents and adult children, siblings, and in-laws. As an ordained minister, I (John) have had the opportunity to work with extended families of all types. I (Margaret) have extensive service as a teacher, mentor, coach, and cheerleader for young parents in our church and community. Together we have been outspoken advocates for the importance of effective parenting.

In this book our primary focus will be on those who have children in the home, while also relating to young adults who are single, engaged, or newlyweds. We feel that we understand your issues because that's where we are in life or where we can still remember being!

It is an honor to work with our more seasoned colleagues, Dave and Claudia. Along with them, we hope to reach across the years and help all generations understand the challenges we all face in our extended family relationships, so that you might discover how to enjoy every season of life in yours.

Together, the four of us want you to know that we are not simply relying on our own understanding. We have tried to give voice to the many hundreds and thousands of people who share our concern for the extended family. Since this is a book about extended families, we went straight to the source: you. Over the past year, we conducted a survey with people throughout the country who are at different stages of family life. In our survey we asked participants to share their joys, concerns, fears, and frustrations, and also to tell us what is working in their extended families. We wanted to know their common concerns and gain helpful tips about what works and what does not work. Whenever possible we will include what many of you have told us.

Also, though we are confident that we read Scripture through "a glass dimly," we do humbly attempt to base our advice on the Bible. In the beginning, God created family, and the foundation for all great civilizations over the years has been the family. The extended family is prominent in the Bible. Families once lived in clans—often as many as 60 to 100 people. Today we call these family clans "the extended family." So throughout this book, we will be referring to biblical principles that will help us relate to our whole family clan now in the twenty-first century.

Our Disclaimer

This book is not about the generational divide or any other kind of divide. It is not about "us" and "them." We are not going to choose sides in some kind of epic battle, because extended family, properly understood, is not about right and wrong or winning and losing. It is about health and harmony. Our hope is that extended families will celebrate the uniquenesses of each member and in doing so build supportive, encouraging relationships.

Extending the family is an art, not a science—there are no fail-safe formulas. But just as the miner searches for diamonds, we can search for and discover precious gems in our own extended family.

Let's get started!

Surveying the Extended Family

What do you think of when you think of being family?

When people think of family, different pictures quickly come to the surface. Some might think narrowly about their own nuclear family of origin—the family that they grew up in. Others might think about the family that they are in presently—especially if there are children in the home. And yet others might be single and even struggle to think in terms of family. Perhaps you have a pleasant image of being family. Maybe you see in your mind the old television show *Leave It to Beaver* with visions of June and Ward Cleaver thoughtfully and successfully guiding Wally and Beaver through the challenges of youth. On the other hand, some might conjure up unpleasant, darker images. Maybe the kooky family of Ozzy Osbourne, which strangely captured the attention of modern America in recent years, comes to mind—*hopefully not!*

In this book we want to challenge you to extend your vision of what you think of when you think of being family to include all the members of your family—not just those who live under your roof. When you think about family, we want you to think about all of your relatives—your parents and grandparents, your in-laws, your uncles and aunts, your cousins, your children and grandchildren. You might also want to include those who are like family—those folk who always have a place at your dinner table and a bed to sleep in whenever they are in town.

THE NEED TO FOCUS ON THE EXTENDED FAMILY

We think it is important to extend your vision of family for three reasons:

First, recent census data show us that fewer and fewer Americans actually live in traditional families. According to recent studies, the traditional nuclear family—a married couple with children in the home—is becoming less common. The *New York Times 2002 Almanac* reports, "The 21st Century American family bears less and less resemblance to the 20th Century American family."[1] In 1960, married couples with children in the home represented 45 percent of the total number of households in America; in 2002, households that had a married couple with children represented only 23.5 percent of the total. Also, the average family size has shrunk to 3.17 persons per household. A startling 31 percent of households with children were headed by a single parent. A significant number of married couples are choosing not to have any children at all. Adult children now are often living at home well into their mid- to late twenties. And an increasing number of children are being raised by grandparents.[2]

Second, we believe that Scripture supports a broad definition of being family. As we previously mentioned, the Old Testament frequently portrays large extended families, consisting of many smaller, nuclear families. During the period of the Judges, the Hebrew people were, in fact, divided into 12 very large tribes or clans. Today at the Passover Seder meal, the youngest child is expected to ask the oldest person present to recite their family story again by asking respectfully, "Why is this night different from the rest?" (What a wonderful intergenerational moment!) In the presence of his mother and his brothers, Jesus refuses to define His family in narrow terms, by claiming that "whoever does the will of my Father in heaven" are members of His family (Matthew 12:50). In some Christian traditions, rightfully and helpfully, folks have long called fellow members of the congregation "brother" or "sister."

And, third, we firmly believe that all families—and *especially* traditional, nuclear families!—need the support of the larger, extended family to thrive. As you will see below, the number-one thing that people in our survey say that they receive from their extended family clan is support and encouragement.

When Sharon Hart Morris's sons were 10 and 12, the unthinkable happened. Her husband, Richard, was killed instantly in a car accident only a few miles from their home. Devastated, Sharon wondered how she would ever be able to pick up the pieces of her life. How could she be both mom and dad to her two boys who were just going into adolescence? Fortunately, Sharon's parents lived nearby and came to her rescue. Here's Sharon's story in her own words:

> The day Richard was killed I was home—I actually remember hearing the sirens as we could hear the interstate from our home—but it was later in the day I got the life-shattering news that my husband was in that accident and did not survive it. Numb and overwhelmed with grief as I was, my parents and the Lord were my comfort. While most parents would give comfort and support during the initial time of crisis, my parents made such a commitment to me that looking back I know what it really means to have family stand in the gap for the long haul. My dad had just retired as Dean of Fuller Seminary. My mom is from Australia, and together they could have relocated to many interesting places around the world, but they chose to stay in the area of California where we lived so they could be there for me and their grandsons. They told me they were committed to helping me raise my sons. They chose to be our adopted "nuclear family." Nana and Papa tried to be as involved in my sons' lives as Richard had been.
>
> The first few months after Richard's death, friends and family brought us meals and my parents joined us for dinners, proving to me and my boys that we still had family. We then got in a pattern of sharing meal preparation. I had Tuesday and Thursday free, so on those days I prepared dinner; the other days Mom was in charge of meals. On the weekends Dad would ask what around the house needed to be fixed. We also shared vacations.
>
> With my parents' support and encouragement, I went back to school to pursue a Ph.D. in clinical psychology. Mom and Dad rearranged their schedules to be available to my boys. Mom would pick up the boys from school, give them snacks, and help with homework. At times she attended parenting meetings in my place.
>
> Dad was there for the markers in my sons' lives. He taught them

how to shave, how to tie a tie, and on their thirteenth and sixteenth birthdays gave them blessings. He was also there in the hard times when the boys were dealing with their anger and trying to make sense out of their dad's death. When things got rough, I could call Dad. Once, one son decided to run away and asked for a ride to Papa's house.

Dad willingly backed up my authority with the boys in the difficult times—like when one son came home with failing grades or another son wanted to pierce his tongue. The boys really respected my dad, and it was great to have a male there to back me up.

Both of my parents were wise in how they helped us without overstepping boundaries. They stayed out of the politics of our family. When one had dyed white hair or a shaved head, they held their tongues. They let us set our own family rules and were true servants—they were my hands and feet—they were there when I needed them. And when I did need them, they bravely spoke up and told me, "I think your boys need you," or "The boys are really tired and you're being a little hard on them." And they faithfully prayed with and for us.

During these years everything wasn't perfect. At times, I imposed too much on them and occasionally they overstepped their roles. We both had to resist letting our feelings get hurt. We worked hard at clearly expressing what we each needed and at problem solving when necessary.

I still need to acknowledge the limits of my parents as they age and I need to continually affirm what they have done and are doing for us. But together we have developed healthy working relationships, and in a large measure my boys and I are emotionally healthy and happy today because of Mom and Dad living out their great commitment to us made five years ago. When tragedy hits, no one can stand in the gap like family.

We say, "Amen!" All types of families need support and encouragement, and the best place to be supported and encouraged is most often in your extended family.

However, you will find that when you broaden your vision of being family to the whole extended family, the picture becomes cloudier and more complicated. As we conducted our national survey, we were able to get a clearer picture of what it means to be extended family and to better understand the real issues extended families are dealing with—and did we ever hit a nerve!

What the Survey Says

We asked people all over the country what comes to mind when they think about extended family. Everybody we heard from—regardless of specific family configuration—seemed to have some kind of strong, emotional reaction when they think of their own extended family. Almost no one was neutral on the subject; rather, we discovered that the phrase "extended family" almost always provoked a wide range of emotions—from joy, happiness, and fulfillment to disappointment, regret, and even anger. Here are a few of the typical responses we received:

- Fun family reunions at the beach
- Christmas at Grandma's house—how it used to be
- My mother-in-law and her demands!
- My daughter-in-law and her catty remarks!
- Aging parents and health problems
- Conflict and disconnection
- Love and security
- My precious grandchildren!
- Pressure, pressure, pressure!
- Manipulative relatives
- A refilled empty nest
- Cousins, aunts and uncles, grandparents, great-grandparents
- Fractured family relationships due to divorce
- Lack of communication
- Family e-mail newsletters and Web site photo updates. I love them!
- Norman Rockwell scenes and other fantasies
- Guilt!

The Best Aspect of Extended Family

In spite of the wide variety of reactions and emotions that we received, there still was considerable agreement on the benefits of relating to your extended family. The following chart shows that encouragement and/or support (dare we say love?) was most frequently listed as the best aspect reported to us. But there are numerous other benefits as well. Extended families also appreciate getting together and having fun, sharing spiritual beliefs, and more.

*What is the **best aspect** of your extended family?*

Support/encouragement	35%
Getting together/having fun	22%
Common spiritual beliefs	11%
Grandchildren	9%
Communication/understanding	8%
Holidays/celebrations/traditions	6%
Tolerance/independence	6%
Not much	3%

Major Tensions in Extended Families

On the other hand, many folks admitted to struggling greatly with some members of their extended families. Read what some consider their greatest concern (or greatest problem) as they strive to relate to all members of their extended family:

- Letting go of failures and mistakes we made while rearing our own children.
- Dealing with our son's addictions and substance abuse.
- Dealing with aging, cranky parents at the same time I have to deal with an adult child in financial trouble.
- Lifestyle choices our son has made that we disapprove of.
- Differing value systems. I don't understand choices our daughter and son-in-law are making, such as giving up time with family in order to work more and have more "stuff."
- Watching one of my grandchildren get punished and verbally abused.
- Going through our 27-year-old daughter's divorce to someone we adored and then her remarriage to an older man with two teenage sons.
- Not feeling connected to our grandchildren who live so far away.
- My daughter is not bringing up my grandchildren in the Christian faith and this greatly concerns me. What can I do?

Complicating the extended family system are the multiple roles we each play. You are probably not just a mother but also a daughter and a sister or a mother-in-law and a niece—or more. (Obviously, the same would apply to men, but we think you get the picture!) Boundaries, power struggles, and conflict with in-laws—which are all related issues, by the way—were listed as the main sources of tension for extended families:

*What are the **major tensions** in your extended family?*

Boundary issues/power struggles/in-laws	21%
Differences in faith/values/beliefs	18%
Communication/conflict	17%
Lack of time together/neglect	9%
Divorce and/or remarriage issues	8%
Financial issues	6%
Aging parents	5%
Geography	5%
Drugs/alcohol	3%
Grandchildren	3%
None	3%
Holidays	2%

Some people thrive in one role and struggle in another. It's no secret that many of us often struggle with the broad category of in-laws. We won't repeat any mother-in-law jokes that reinforce negative stereotypes because we have uncovered some very painful situations. One frustrated survey participant wrote:

I am a 37-year-old female, wife, mother, and daughter-in-law. My greatest stress is with my in-laws, specifically my mother- and father-in-law, and their daughters (both married with three kids each). While these are my responses, my husband (the son and brother) would agree with most everything I have put down because our extended family relationships are a periodic topic of discussion and perpetual problem!

The major tension in our extended family comes from my bossy, selfish sisters-in-law (both are younger than their brother, my husband) and my mother-in-law. My mother-in-law is well-meaning but is so controlling and manipulative I can't stand to be around her. Both my mother-in-law and father-in-law disapproved of our marriage. My husband and I suspect that his divorce from his first wife (who ran off with his best friend) is an unspoken tension on his family's side, especially with his sisters—perhaps shame on their part in having a divorced brother. Fortunately, our marriage is alive and well, but no thanks to support from my husband's family!

You asked how we resolve extended family conflicts. That's the problem—we don't! It's kind of hard when one or another member refuses to communicate with you for six-plus months at a time. But the best way I've found to communicate with our extended family is through e-mail or writing letters. Talking doesn't work well because others tend to interrupt, override, and don't have or make time to listen, even on the nonconfrontational issues. They are driving me crazy!

The Best Ways Extended Families Communicate

The best way to deal with boundary issues is clear communication, so we asked our survey participants what is the best way to communicate. The responses were not surprising: Alexander Graham Bell's invention—the telephone—remains the most popular form of communication, but, sadly, people also told us that they tried to avoid communication with their extended family or that they only communicated with their extended family through a third party. Here is what they wrote:

What is the best way to **communicate** *with your extended family?*

Telephone	44%
In person	21%
E-mail	20%
Written notes/cards	6%
Very carefully	6%
Avoidance	2%
Through a third party	1%

What Pulls Extended Families Together

Not only does good, clear communication help bring families together, but so do certain events. Surprisingly, tragedy (e.g., funerals, illnesses) was ranked as the number-one thing that pulls extended families together. We were pleased to learn that most people (but certainly not all) feel that in tough times they can count on their families to pull together and work through the tragic circumstances.

*What kinds of things **pull you together**?*

Tragedy/illness/deaths/funerals	31%
Celebrations/birthdays/weddings	21%
Holidays/traditions	19%
Reunions/family visits	11%
Vacations/travel	5%
Grandchildren	4%
Spiritual values/faith/church	4%
Meals together	3%
Recreation/sports	2%

Extended Families' Favorite Activities

We were also interested in what families like to do when they gather, so if you are the one planning the gathering, you might want to read this list carefully! Here are the tabulated results of our nationwide survey:

*What are your **favorite extended-family activities**?*

Holidays together	28%
Meals together	21%
Vacations/family trips/camping	14%
Birthdays/weddings	12%
Reunions/family gatherings	10%
Playing games together	7%
Sports/sporting events	4%
Movies/shopping	3%
Church	1%

"Now that I am about to become a mother-in-law, I'd like to be a great one and avoid the many pitfalls I experienced with my own in-laws and those I see in the families around me. I don't want to be the mother-in-law I had."

—SURVEY RESPONDENT

Challenges Along the Way

As we compiled our survey results, we concluded that there are seven basic challenges of building positive extended family relationships, and that their mastery will lead you to improving your relationships with members of your extended family.

The first challenge is to *develop realistic expectations and a clear vision* for your extended family. The Bible says that where there is no vision, the people perish (Proverbs 29:18, KJV)—and so it is with the extended family. In this challenge, we will look at different components that complicate extended family relationships. You will see that coming up with a realistic vision is a challenge! Most people have either no vision or an unrealistic vision for what the extended family might be.

The second challenge is to *move beyond chitchat and learn to speak the truth in love.* In our counseling sessions, our seminars, our survey, and our own personal experience, good communication is often hard to achieve. Many families settle for simple chitchat—rehearsing the same old conversations about the same old boring but safe subjects year after year. In this challenge we help you move beyond small talk to fulfill the biblical challenge of learning "to speak the truth in love." You will see that this is not easy to do and requires great spiritual discipline.

You will discover, however, that once you have a clear vision for a close and healthy extended family and once you try to move beyond chitchat, conflict and/or uneasy disagreements will erupt from time to time. These should not necessarily be considered a negative development: Reasonable minds will disagree, as they say. However, you will want to develop some skills for managing conflict and for dealing with disagreements in a way that does not lead to hostility. Therefore, the third challenge is to *be civil, calm, and clear when you disagree.*

Our fourth challenge—*promoting harmony when you get together*—is geared more specifically toward particular family gatherings. In this section, we try to give you good, practical tips for how to make those traditional get-togethers meaningful. What makes for a good vacation? What kinds of events pull us closer together as extended families, and what tends to pull us apart? You might be surprised!

In the fifth challenge, we turn our attention to various and specific relationships—*relationships between grandparents and grandchildren, or relationships with aunts and uncles, cousins, or adult siblings.* Sometimes relationships develop naturally because you live in the same neighborhood with other relatives, but more often close relationships with specific extended family members require work and are the result of an intentional decision to build those relationships.

In this book we do not want to give anyone the impression that all problems can be solved or that every family experiences the Hollywood happy ending. The Bible informs us, "In all things God works for the good of those who love him" (Romans 8:28), but sinful behavior has painful consequences. *How do you learn to deal with the hard issues?* is our sixth challenge. This chapter will be helpful to those not looking for quick and easy fixes to family problems but instead seeking coping strategies.

And finally, we believe that it is important to *understand and respect boundaries and to extend ourselves beyond family.* When we are involved in reaching out to others and pursuing interests beyond our own family, we can find balance in our extended family relationships and also have a life of our own. And within our families we need to know how to extend our web of care beyond our immediate family. Where does your family end and your extended family begin? When do you draw a financial boundary or declare that enough is enough? Understanding where and when to draw lines with others is a difficult but important lesson to learn in life, and we want to help you do it with your own family.

With these seven challenges in mind as your guideposts, it's time to start our extended family adventure. You may want to work through this book alone or with others in your extended family. You could use this book as a catalyst for great conversations at your next family get-together. We hope it will be an avenue for open discussion and discovery and will foster better relationships between parents, children, grandparents, and all those who are part of your family clan.

QUESTIONS FOR REFLECTION

To begin the adventure, we suggest that you reflect on the following questions, keeping in mind that your extended family includes parents, grandparents, adult children, grandchildren, in-laws, siblings, aunts, uncles, cousins, nephews, nieces, and so on.

1. What is the best aspect of your extended family?

2. What are the major tensions in your extended family?

3. How do you resolve extended-family conflicts?

4. What is the best way to communicate with your extended family?

5. What are your favorite extended-family activities?

6. What tends to pull you together as a family?

Part Two

Seven Challenges of Relating to the Extended Family

Having Realistic Expectations

The Scott family wakes up the Friday after Thanksgiving to discover that their plans for a hike and picnic together will not work with the torrential downpour outside. So, Gloria—the grandmother and matriarch—decides it will be best to "divide and conquer." Since this day is the biggest shopping day of the year, she will take her two daughters and daughter-in-law Christmas shopping while Paul—the grandfather and patriarch—and his sons, son-in-law, and future son-in-law will take the grandchildren and stepgrandchildren-to-be out for pizza and to Blockbuster to select a classic movie the entire family can enjoy together. At the last moment, Sean and his friend Rafael pass on Blockbuster and head for the closest gym.

Paul arrives at Blockbuster only to discover that J. Paul Jr. plans to remain in the car to finish his vitally important cell phone conversation. Once the group—comprising Paul, son-in-law Steve, future son-in-law Bill, and seven grandchildren ranging in ages from 14 to 4—steps inside the Blockbuster it becomes apparent that the task ahead may not be so easy. Checkout lines snake through several aisles of the store, and judging from the number of customers present it seems highly unlikely that the New Releases section will yield much, if anything.

Nevertheless, Paul forges ahead and emits the cry of a grandparent determined to make everyone happy: "Let's find a movie all of us will like." Almost immediately four grandchildren rush to the games section and find games they are dying to try. Two other grandchildren head straight for the cartoon section while the remaining grandchild wants to know if he can watch an R-rated movie. Steve explodes and suggests that they should just forget the movie idea—no kid of his is going to watch an R-rated movie— so why don't they just watch the football games on television? Bill explains that his theory on parenting allows children to fully express themselves and explore the adult world through their movie choices. Paul is getting a serious migraine but soldiers on with the sure and certain knowledge that Gloria will consider anything less than the entire family watching a movie together— complete with popcorn and hot chocolate—a failure.

An hour and a half later Paul is headed home with $72.80 less in his wallet, a rental Nintendo and three games, one VHS classic movie, one DVD new release, and an assortment of boxes of candy and two hideous bags of multicolor cotton candy. He has bargained his way through the process and considers himself extremely fortunate to have brokered a deal where everyone agrees to watch the classic movie together in exchange for their freedom to play video games, watch the new DVD, or switch back and forth between bowl games once the movie is over. He even half believes that Gloria won't find out how much the classic family movie rental fiasco actually cost.

If simply choosing a movie to watch together can be so complicated, just imagine what's happening on the shopping trip with Gloria and her daughters and daughter-in-law, who all have different styles and tastes. On this day it becomes clear that the Scotts need to work on having realistic expectations and understanding one another. Maybe you do too.

UNDERSTANDING YOUR OWN FAMILY CLAN

Unlike the nuclear family, the structure of most extended families is all over the map. Everyone is part of an extended family—even if it is an adopted family. Some folks are single and have never been married, while others are widowed. Some are married with older kids and others have infants in diapers. These differences can cause many complications—especially when the gang gets together like the Scotts' Thanksgiving reunion. Let's consider five areas of generational expectations that might help the Scotts better understand their own extended family.

Spanning Generations and Cultures

An important dynamic at work in any extended family is the generational and cultural expectations. In America, sociologists have identified distinct characteristics for the World War II generation, the Silent Generation, Baby Boomers, Generation X, and now Generation Y or Echo Boomers.

Different generational expectations reveal themselves in the approach to everyday life, such as food and dining preferences. A younger child might think macaroni and cheese is awesome, while the same food might remind older folks of hard times when they ate macaroni and cheese every night because it was cheap. Some might have the "waste not, want not" mind-set of Depression-era people versus the modern "when in doubt, throw it out" mentality. Younger families may cook less and eat out more frequently than do older ones. There is no easy way to work within these generational preferences, but they must be respected.

Sometimes the older generation may not understand the importance of acknowledging that their adult children are indeed adults. For instance, Martha, at age 52, is still controlled by her mother. She checks in daily with her mother, and if she misses a day, her mother lets her know about it. Major holidays are a command performance.

And then there's Millie's story. "Within two minutes, she reduced me to a 10-year-old!" Millie said. "I should feel very grown up—I'm over 50 and have married children myself, but when I'm around my mom, I instantly become the child."

Millie laughingly related a recent conversation with her mother. "Millie, I just don't know what will ever happen to your brother," her mom said.

Millie responded, "Mom, he's 56 years old. He's already happened!"

Millie said she didn't want someday to be an 83-year-old parent standing at the sink saying, "I don't know what will ever happen to my 60-year-old son and daughter-in-law!" While we know "the children" is an endearing term, adult offspring probably would rather not be identified as such. That's their reasonable generational expectation.

Cultural differences can create generational misunderstandings as well. "It wasn't until after we were married that I realized culture would be a major issue in my relationship with my mother-in-law." Lisa married into a Japanese-American family. Her husband, Frank, seemed all-American. They got along great—it was Frank's mother whom Lisa found hard to relate to. Lisa explained, "Frank's mother was interned during World War II. Her family lost everything they owned and after the war had to start completely over. My mother-in-law to this day is fearful of losing everything again. That explains her tendency to be so obsessive-compulsive. For instance, she saves everything and hoards for the future. Her kitchen pantry looks like a bomb shelter for the whole town! She has enough food for an army. She also has enough clothes to dress a battalion. Many items are unused with the price tag still attached."

Lisa's challenge was to understand her in-laws' culture. Once she understood how her mother-in-law grew up and how devastating it must have been to be interned right here in America, it helped her to be more tolerant and understanding. Even if your in-laws are the same nationality as you, there may be other, more subtle cultural differences. Your in-laws may be from a different part of the country. Or they're contemporary, you're traditional; they're city, you're rural. Whatever the situation, you need to be aware and be sensitive.

Financial Demographics

Different economic levels and choices abound in extended families. Some families choose to scrape by on one salary in order to have one parent at home with the kids, while others decide that two incomes are necessary to provide for the kind of lifestyle they desire. Some couples are DINKs (dual income no kids) who often seem to have plenty of disposable income, yet in these turbulent times the sudden shock of unemployment can crimp checkbooks. Others are single and may or may not live with their parents. They may be financially secure or still somewhat dependent upon their parents.

Time and money are often trade-offs. J. Paul Jr. gives large sums of money to charitable causes; Jan can barely afford the mortgage and the utility bill but gives much of her time to her church and the PTA. Neither one is better or right; they merely exhibit different ways of approaching the resources of time and money.

Some, like Paul Sr., decide to retire early while others are not able to do so. Going out to a ball game or a movie may not be a big deal financially to one family but might present a hardship to another family. Just as people operate on different economic levels, they also put different economic values on things: One family may spend a great deal of money on fine dining but think the greens fees at the golf course are too high. Another family might think nothing of spending a small fortune in a bookstore but refuse to spend any money to ride bumper cars on a family outing. Healthy extended families recognize and respect economic choices.

Spiritual Journey

Many extended families experience faith differences. Within a typical Christian extended family various levels of commitment, faith, and church involvement can be found. Some grandparents have definite expectations for how their grandchildren should be raised and for their spiritual development. Our survey elicited such opposite responses: "My grandson is two years old and still isn't baptized!" to "Can you believe my son and daughter-in-law actually baptized my granddaughter as a baby? That's not the way we do it in our church!" to "I was so disappointed my parents didn't make the effort to come to our baby's baptism. Why can't they be more interested in their grandson?"

Extended families today in America often include at least one member from a non-Christian religion. These differences can be quite painful and, if not addressed, can become the source of significant tension.

The Scotts struggle with this issue on the Sunday after Thanksgiving. Jan and Steve invite everyone to accompany them to the new church that meets in the elementary school building. J. Paul Jr. and Julia say that Kaitlin and Trey are welcome to go with their cousins, but they will be going to brunch and to an art gallery. Sean does not feel comfortable with Jan and Steve's brand of Christianity and thinks he will go to an early service at a liturgical church. Hayley says Sunday is her only day to sleep in and she really needs the extra rest. Gloria and Paul would much prefer to go to their own traditional church but agree to go with Jan and Steve's choice. Such a Sunday can be the source of conflict—or it can become the creative fuel for a rich discussion later that evening of what they all experienced that day and what it meant to them personally.

It is safe to assume that we are all on a faith journey and that we are all at different places. Learning to deal openly and honestly with family members whose faith journey does not parallel our own is one of the more important keys to successful extended families. We will write more on this delicate issue in Challenge Six.

Where and How Closely You Live

Today many extended families are spread out geographically. Families may not live in the same town or state or country and may see each other face-to-face only once or twice a year. Other extended families live within a 25-mile radius and talk to each other daily. The Scotts have family who live both close by and far away. Each scenario offers unique challenges in understanding and dealing with family expectations.

When we (Dave and Claudia) were first married, we moved to Germany at the invitation of Uncle Sam. Claudia's parents were crushed. When she was growing up, Claudia's grandmother and aunt lived next door; to live halfway around the world was just unthinkable for her parents.

Dave's parents were happy for us. Growing up in a military family, Dave lived in many different places and rarely around any of his extended family. Our experiences could not have been more different! Actually, our move to

---

"We can't seem to keep both sets of grandparents happy. They both want more time with the grandchildren."

—A YOUNGER SURVEY RESPONDENT

"It is extremely stressful that our grandchildren are being raised differently from the way we raised their parents."

—AN OLDER SURVEY RESPONDENT

"I have to bite my tongue. I can't really express my thoughts or feelings to my parents. They still want me to obey whatever they say, but somehow, some way, we have to grow up. They need to let go and let us be the parents."

—A YOUNGER SURVEY RESPONDENT

Germany helped us get off on the right foot with our extended family. We were able to establish our own marriage without the complication of having family close by. Now our own children and grandchildren live all over the United States, and the closest family is 200 miles away.

As our extended family (John and Margaret's) dwell in three different time zones, telecommunications companies love us! In our home with our two teenage daughters, we have four cell phones, two land lines, six e-mail addresses, three voice messaging systems, caller ID, and one plain old-fashioned mailbox at the front of our house. One would think we are easy to contact, but we are told that is not always true.

Connecting with our extended family requires intentional coordination. First, our extended family schedules are all different and subject to change without notice. A good time to talk for one household may be a moment of chaos for another. Being on mountain standard time means that we are often at soccer practice or the orthodontist or at church meetings when our relatives on eastern standard time are ready to catch up on the phone. And, of course, we do not pick up any popularity points when we call after our dishes are done in the evening only to find that they *were* asleep!

Also, difficulties may arise when different communication patterns are preferred. For example, one family may communicate virtually everything by e-mail, while another family may not even have access to a computer. Or one sibling may call another family member two or three times a week from a cell phone, while another contacts others sporadically through lengthy, well-written epistles sent "snail mail." Learning to work within different communication patterns over the miles is crucial for healthy extended families.

Families who live in the same town may also experience misunderstandings and unrealistic expectations. One survey participant answered the question "What is the best aspect of your extended family?" with, "We all live in the same town." Then she answered the next question, "What is the greatest stress in your extended family?" with, "We all live in the same town." Unrealistic expectations often arise around issues such as child care—how much are grandparents involved—and time commitments—such as getting together for dinner each Sunday after church.

The years we (John and Margaret) were fortunate enough to live in the same town as our extended family, we fell into the pattern of eating at the same restaurant every Sunday night together. It became such an enjoyable and relaxing time that we cannot even remember how that habit started or when it became a firmly entrenched tradition. But for every happy story like ours, many others struggle with having realistic expectations, whether family lives near or far away.

Who's in Charge?

Who makes the ultimate decisions in your extended family? Is your family decision-making structure a monarchy, an oligarchy, or a democracy? Many times the older generation like Paul and Gloria tends to follow a patriarchal pattern in which the oldest adult male is in charge and normally is accustomed to calling the shots. Sometimes it is a strong-willed female or matriarch. Younger families may tend to be more democratic—one person, one vote! Single people such as Sean Scott and his friend Rafael are not in the habit of having to consult others before they make significant decisions.

Other times the world's golden rule applies: The one with the most gold makes the rules! In our example above, one can certainly imagine J. Paul Jr. trying to coax everybody to vote for his favorite restaurant by promising to pick up the tab—something Jan's family would not be able to do. This is not a healthy pattern.

When extended families gather, leadership expectations occasionally clash. Does the oldest living person decide where the whole family is going to dinner? Or do all votes count, including that of the dog? We have found

---

It is possible to make extended families work when you live near one another. Kevin and Sarah Jenkins have three sons, ages 4, 8, and 10, and live in the same town with Sarah's parents and her two sisters and their families. Kevin and Sarah took the initiative in getting the family together and talking about their expectations, and they worked out the following plan: They decided to have dinner together every Thursday night. Among family members, the host or hostess changes every week, and the meal can be Chinese take-out, delivery pizza, or a home-cooked entrée. What matters the most is that they have the opportunity to check in with one another and be together—but it probably wouldn't have happened if Sarah and Kevin hadn't taken the initiative.

from our own experience in counseling couples that this is often the most difficult and unspoken source of conflict in extended family gatherings. Here, give-and-take is especially necessary or the result might be anarchy!

The Wilson family during one holiday together spontaneously decided to go out for Starbucks coffee. As they were waiting in line, they began to discuss who was going to pick up the bill. What started as friendly competition became a duel between Mr. Wilson, the patriarch of the family, and Rick, his son-in-law, who was tired of his father-in-law's always being in control and paying for everything. Besides, he felt his father-in-law didn't approve of his profession as a teacher and probably didn't think he could even afford to buy a cup of coffee for everyone.

This family outing could have gone much better if they had discussed beforehand whose treat it would be. Perhaps if Rick had initially offered to pay, his father-in-law would have graciously accepted his generosity. Another option would have been to go dutch, with each picking up his own check.

If at all possible we encourage you to share the leadership. Even if you have a strong patriarch or matriarch in the family, extended families need many who are willing to share responsibilities and, from time to time, take the leadership. Don't assume that the oldest person or the person whose home is the gathering place must always assume responsibility for everything.

Some family leaders are born, some are made, and others grow into the job with age or experience. The important thing is to take responsibility for doing what you do best to help the extended family create happy memories. Even young children can and should be given opportunities to develop their leadership within the extended family.

Start by recognizing your own leadership style and offering to use your strengths for the good of the entire extended family. Maybe you really like taking the initiative in choosing restaurants, renting a beach cottage, planning a family reunion, or planning a picnic from site selection to menu choice. These are all possibilities for positive, proactive family leadership.

Once when Margaret's parents were planning to visit, they were having difficulty finding economical flights. Margaret, who is Internet savvy, went online, found dirt-cheap flights, and called her dad and said, "Dad, what's your credit card number? I found you really cheap flights to come to Denver for Thanksgiving and if you want me to, I'll book them right now!"

Margaret's parents were so pleased that she had taken the lead in checking airline ticket prices. For them, it would have been a real hassle. (Dave and Claudia say any time their kids want to book flights for them, they have their bags packed.)

An important facet of the leadership role is what to plan to do for fun when the entire extended family gathers. You can take the initiative in exploring new recreational activities—try something nobody has done before. Find the neutral ground. Go on and take some leadership—at the very least there will come some wonderful new family stories about the experience.

What happens when we misunderstand one another and when our expectations are not met or are totally unrealistic? Hurt feelings ensue. Misunderstandings happen. Relationships strain. As we said previously, relationships are hard to maintain even when you're together daily in your nuclear family. Healthy extended-family relationships will require frequent doses of forgiveness, acceptance, and understanding.

LOVING YOU JUST THE WAY YOU ARE

Someone once said, "Just because someone doesn't love you the way you want them to, doesn't mean they don't love you with all they have." What a great thought to apply to the extended family. If we realized that the irritating people in our family tree just may be loving us to the best of their ability, perhaps we would be more forgiving. And what if they don't love us to their full capacity? If we want to have a relationship with them in the future, we need to be willing to forgive and accept whatever the present circumstances are. To make extended family work requires us to be adults. We assume that is why you are reading this book—that you want better family relationships. If so, the first step is to forgive and accept those in your family who drive you crazy.

Forgiveness Begins with You

A survey participant expressed the following: "I could forgive my mother-in-law, but it wouldn't make any difference because she would never reciprocate or be willing to change or have a relationship with me. She hates me." No one ever said extended family is easy. But we believe this daughter-in-law is not powerless and that there are actions she can take. On her own she can ask for forgiveness and forgive her mother-in-law regardless of how her mother-in-law responds.

Forgiveness in the extended family works differently than in a nuclear family or husband-wife relationship. In a marriage you need both forgiveness and reconciliation for the marriage to grow and be healthy. In an extended family, sometimes all you can do is seek forgiveness and forgive others. You can't make reconciliation happen. But the first step is to forgive. Amazingly, we've discovered that when we are willing to forgive in our own hearts, even if we are not reconciled, time can heal the ugly stuff. Hopefully, we don't have to live day in and day out with those in our extended family with whom we are estranged by lack of reconciliation. But even if that is the case, we can trust our heavenly Father to give us the grace and patience to endure.

Our section on forgiveness would not be complete without acknowledging the great power of prayer. It's hard to continually pray for people and still dislike them. We encourage you to pray daily for those in your family with whom you do not have a good relationship. We are told in the Scriptures to pray for our enemies. While we wouldn't want to consider anyone in our extended families an enemy, certainly this biblical admonition to pray also applies to irritating family members.

Once we're willing to forgive others in our family, we need to take the next step and accept our extended family as a package deal.

Accepting and Understanding

When we're willing to practice forgiveness, we can truly seek to understand and appreciate the unique individuals who make up our extended family. Often it's the ways we're different that are the basis for misunderstandings. Our differences do have the potential to divide us, but our challenge is to respect and learn from each other while celebrating the strengths that God has given each of us. Differences are inevitable, whatever they may be— lifestyles, values, faith, family structure, or personality. It's important that we learn to accept and love unconditionally in our relationships with other

---

"To grow up, it is necessary to forgive your parents. When you do not forgive them it means you are clinging to them in the hope that if you can make them feel guilty enough they will finally come through with more parenting."[1]

family members who have made decisions that differ from those we would have made.

Sometimes the decisions and choices others make involve moral issues and even harm others. How can you love and accept unconditionally when you disapprove of the behavior? Listen to this mother's story:

"My son has chosen to reject God and to live a lifestyle that is contrary to my Christian beliefs. I still love him and want to accept him without condoning his behavior, but the pain I suffer at times is almost unbearable. I'm hurting. Does anyone really know or care? When I feel so alone, I try to pray and commit to God my feelings of frustration, fear, and a great sense of failure as a parent. When my son visits me, I tell him that I love him, but I state clearly that I don't condone his behavior. And when I get on the lecture circuit and catch myself nagging him to the point that I see him withdrawing, I try to ask him to forgive me. I find that I also have to forgive myself and confess my anger to God for not changing my son."

While this mother's pain is very real, she is seeking to maintain the relationship with her son without approving his behavior. Yes, it's a fine line between accepting the person and condoning the behavior, but didn't Jesus model this in His conversation with the Samaritan woman at the well? He didn't condone her past, but in pursuing the conversation He helped her think about her future. Likewise, this mother, in her attempts to continue to accept, love, and relate to her son, is keeping the lines of communication open so she can influence him in the future.

As you begin to be more intentional in forgiving and accepting family members for who they are, realize that they may also be in a different season of life than you. When push comes to shove, be willing to defer to others. Family is about understanding—not just being understood. When you focus

---

Let us encourage you to never end a family relationship—even if you feel deep hurts from past offenses by family members. Realize over time things change. If you cut off the relationship and refuse reconciliation, the seeds of bitterness will remain and your heart will harden. Your anger and frustration will not go away just because you refuse to forgive or seek forgiveness.

on forgiving, accepting, and understanding those in your extended family, you will be better equipped to create a realistic vision for the future.

CREATING A REALISTIC VISION FOR YOUR OWN EXTENDED FAMILY

Whatever the present state of your relationships, you can take steps today to build better connections with others in your extended family. No matter what the past, healthy family relationships are definitely worth exerting your best effort. One of the great rewards of a healthy extended family is the sure and certain knowledge that you have others in your tribe to divide the sorrows and multiply the celebrations of life together. If you want to foster better extended family relationships and have realistic expectations, consider one last suggestion: *Let it begin with you.*

Take the Initiative

Our best advice for those who want to create a realistic vision for their extended family is to be an activist. Don't wait for someone else—like your parents or your adult children—to take the initiative. Visualize what you wish for your extended family, verbalize your expectations, and work toward achieving them.

If you live in the same town, plan a weekly or monthly get-together. Create a circular e-mail or family newsletter that reaches all generations. Set a regular time to call family members.

Show an interest in family members, especially those who are different from you. Be nonjudgmental in your approach to learning new information.

What about parents and grandparents who don't embrace new technology? Perhaps you would like them to become more computer literate so you can correspond by e-mail or enjoy a family Web page. Maybe someday they will, but in the meantime be patient and stay connected through phone calls, letters, and visits.

—JOHN AND MARGARET

Be inquisitive. Ask lots of questions and really listen. Be honest. If you are surprised or befuddled, say so. Plan family get-togethers with siblings and also with parents and grandparents.

We have discovered that many of the problems in our own extended families occur simply because of our own unrealistic expectations and lack of effort. Laura grew up in a family who always wrote thank-you notes. She tried to instill this in her two sons. The Christmas rule was "Write your thank-you notes, then you can play with or use your gift." Both boys married into families where the women did the gift shopping and holiday correspondence. However, one daughter-in-law grew up in a family where a verbal thank-you was sufficient.

Each Christmas, tension mounted as Laura got only a flippant "thanks" as presents were opened—or if they weren't together for Christmas, sometimes she didn't get *any* acknowledgement of the gifts. She became irritated that her son and daughter-in-law didn't take the time to write her a proper thank-you note after she spent so much time choosing presents for them. Realistically, this pattern will probably not change in the future, and this may be one expectation that Laura may need to just let go.

We are convinced that whatever your present relationship with your parents, adult children, grandchildren, and in-laws, you can be intentional about working toward building closer relationships. The desire to be close to our relatives is not enough. We've learned that we must talk and stay in touch because people change. One caution: Realize that even close, healthy rela-

---

Understand where your expectations come from by processing your history with your own parents and in-laws. Is your relationship with your own parents and in-laws positive or negative? If they have passed away, what was your relationship like before they died? Those relationships have a direct bearing on how you relate to the younger generation. If we were not affirmed and supported growing up, we may slip back into looking to others for affirmation and approval as if we were still children. If we were manipulated emotionally, we may unintentionally do the same to others. You might need to go beyond the examples of the family in your life and choose different role models to follow.

tionships will not be as intimate as they probably were in your own nuclear family before it extended. Now is the time to accept that reality and say, "Hey, that's okay. We'll take whatever closeness we can get."

While you have little direct control over your extended family, you can control your own actions and attitudes. So look at what you can control and what you can do to make your extended-family relationships great.

We hope our suggestions for meeting the challenge to create a realistic vision for your family will help you get off to a good start in understanding and relating to your own extended family. One last suggestion: Be brave enough to engage the generations in your family to talk together about your vision for your family. You may have some great conversations and be amazed at what you discover. At any rate, your time together as an extended family will not be boring!

Moving Beyond Chitchat

When your family clan gets together, what do you talk about? If you are like the Scott family, you will have a few safe topics to which everybody in the family can contribute. The Scotts are avid football and soccer fans, so sports talk is always a safety net. Although safe subjects differ from family to family, you probably know those comfortable topics: the weather, general health, diet and/or exercise programs, the latest headlines in the papers, sports scores, or maybe the latest fashion trends. We are sure that you can make your own extended-family list.

Many possible interesting and enriching topics of conversation exist, but we must work to find them. Ernest Bramah once wrote, "Although there exist many thousand subjects for elegant conversation, there are persons who cannot meet a cripple without talking about feet."[1] Hopefully, we can all move beyond the obvious, safe topics of conversation, into areas that make us all better people, binding our families together. Deeper conversations can take place if you are willing to wade into deeper water. Obviously, risk is involved, but if these conversations are crafted carefully and proper boundaries are observed, the rewards can be great.

Then there are those forbidden topics—things about which nobody is allowed to speak. In the play *Cheaper by the Dozen*, those forbidden topics of discussion are termed neutrally "Eskimo." These are topics of conversation that often receive a frown and get people sent off to their rooms early after dinner but that you *never* talk about.

Other topics are like lighting rods. One only has to bring them up to start a heated discussion that soon becomes negative. So how can family members connect with loving and honest conversation that goes deeper than chitchat? That's the challenge we will be considering in the following pages.

We'll start by looking at the lighter conversations—actually, at times chitchat may be appropriate. Then we'll look at how we can go deeper in our conversations while avoiding some obvious potholes. We'll consider how we can connect across the generations and speak the truth in love. We don't have to choose between honesty and peace. Next we'll give you some practical tips for connecting with deeper conversations while staying positive. Speaking the truth in love isn't always easy and may be hard work, but open, honest communication will translate into deeper, more loving family relationships. Family discussions need not remain superficial and boring!

SAFE TALK: CHITCHAT AND "SOUTHERN GUSH"

Everybody—from the oldest to the youngest—can and probably will weigh in with their opinion on the safe subjects. These topics are generally safe because even when people disagree, it's no big deal—no one really cares too much or for too long. For example, who really cares deeply when one person looks up into the sky and says, "I think its going to rain," only to hear another say, "No, the wind is coming out of the west. I don't think it will rain today"? It would be silly to get into a fight about the weather that even the experts with lots of expensive equipment cannot always accurately predict! Everyone, however, has an opinion on the weather and will gladly share it.

But just talking about the weather is boring. And it is also boring to run over the same old tired, safe subjects—what we call chitchat—year after year after year. In our survey results, one of the top frustrations when family gets together was dealing with the huge amount of idle, seemingly meaningless conversation. Survey participants repeatedly asked, "How do we move beyond small talk to have deeper and more meaningful discussions with our extended family?"

One of the respondents to the survey said that she would like to learn how to move past what she called "southern gush." We thought that was a striking phrase. Since all four of us have lived in the South, we know exactly what she meant; we imagine that you understand that term as well. And though we now know "gush" is not exclusively southern, any excessive gush or chitchat can be detrimental.

In fact, here we are reminded of a humorous short story with a very serious kick. In *A Good Man Is Hard to Find*, Flannery O'Connor writes about a grandmother who apparently loves chitchat. She talks incessantly about nothing to her extended family as they travel by automobile through Georgia on their way to Florida. Her behavior drives the grandchildren nuts and causes all the others to fall silent. Unfortunately, they have a single-car accident on a rural route. Their car rolls over into a ditch. The grandmother continues to chatter away. Then, their would-be rescuers turn out to be dangerous convicts—murderers!—who have escaped from the local penitentiary. Even though she recognizes them from their photographs in the paper, she continues to carry on a polite conversation with them while the convicts proceed to steal their clothes and their car, before murdering the entire family.[2] The ending of the story is tragic, but the grandmother's capacity for chitchat under extreme duress stands as an everlasting testimony to the power of southern gush.

Sometimes small talk can be a family saver. We have experienced those times when we started down the path of deeper, richer conversation only to be drawn into unhealthy arguments that contain discouraging disagreements. Verbal spats can ruin family gatherings and family relationships. This occurs generally when truth telling is done at the wrong time or with the wrong motivation. In fact, there are some times when chitchat is proper. At Thanksgiving dinner, when the cook asks about the sweet potato pie, you should probably say something like "It's fine!" no matter how it tastes. (One of us learned this one the hard way early in marriage!)

When emerging from an extended family "cold war," small talk may be called upon to break the silence. When trust has been broken, chitchat may be necessary—and is to be preferred to silence—until open, honest lines of communication can be restored.

Recently, the Sloan family experienced firsthand the importance of choosing chitchat in order to preserve their relationship with their 25-year-old son, Ben. Regarded as perhaps the black sheep of the Sloan family, Ben, after graduating from college, moved to California—away from family. Ben's parents, Bob and Linda, are upstanding members of the community, committed church members, dedicated volunteers, and part of a large extended family in a small Midwestern town.

Ben has inherited his parents' trait of standing up for what you believe; however, Ben believes that the legalization of marijuana is a vitally important and relevant issue. Bob and Linda cannot even imagine the possibility of discussing this issue when Ben visits for Christmas and the entire extended family is together. Bob and Linda decided that this is a highly charged emotional issue upon which they and their son will most likely never agree. Any serious discussion of it during Ben's visit could wreak family havoc. Thus, they decide to avoid this particular issue during the visit and select safe topics ahead of time in order to stay in relationship with Ben and preserve the opportunity for a deeper conversation at a more appropriate time.

Avoiding Communication Potholes

One caution: Some extended families members do not necessarily have the welfare of the extended family at heart when they attempt to entice the family into a conversation on a potentially controversial issue. In your own extended family, can you think of someone who tends to be insensitive to the feelings of others or at times is simply unhappy and looks for a verbal confrontation?

When Ruthie and her sister-in-law Kendra get together, sparks usually fly. They can argue over little things like the theological implication of *Tele-*

Wedding weekends can be an excellent time to engage in both chitchat and southern gush. We heartily recommend that you gush about the bride's dress and the groom's plans and just about everything else! Emotions are generally on edge during wedding weekends. Much time and money have been invested for one purpose. In our experience, wedding weekends should be approached with great caution and are not the time to revisit old arguments or to resolve family difficulties. Chitchat may be enough. Simple civility counts a great deal.

tubbies or what television programs and/or videos are appropriate for young children. It's almost as if Ruthie is being the antagonist and is trying to provoke an argument with Kendra. Or consider the strained relationship between siblings and siblings-in-law in the Henderson family. They hold different political views, and when they are together you can count on one or two not-so-friendly political debates. Since most families tend to have at least one antagonist, here are two tips for avoiding unproductive confrontations:

Avoid being an annoying conversationalist. An annoying conversationalist looks for the first available opportunity to blurt out an opinion and draw others into an argument. Perhaps you have family members who are consistently annoying. Beware! You may unknowingly be that person.

Avoid encouraging the family antagonist. You may not always want to take the bait of the family antagonist. When this family member makes an extreme comment like, "You can't tell me ..." or "You will never find another (fill in the blank) as good as this," or "He/She is the best (fill in the blank) in the county/city/state/nation/world," he is floating his agenda. First of all, he may actually believe his statement because he thinks he *is* that smart—which may simply be because many people choose wisely not to argue with him. Second, he may be waiting to see who has the guts to argue and be genuinely interested in debating his opinion. Or he may be looking for a fight he feels sure he will win. Whether it is about politics, sports, religion, cars, or weather, think before you respond to the family antagonist's extreme statements.

CONNECTING ACROSS THE GENERATIONS

A few years ago, I (John) had the privilege of taking my then 12-year-old daughter, Megan, to see her 95-year-old great-grandmother. Since we lived in different parts of the country, Megan had not seen her great-grandmother in a couple of years. Naturally, we were both excited about the visit, but I must admit that I was wary about what a 12-year-old would talk about with a 95-year-old over a lengthy afternoon and evening visit. Although they were related as great-grandmother and great-granddaughter, in others ways they were strangers since they had not been in close contact. To help Megan, we went over a list of safe topics in the car moments before we arrived in case we hit a lull in the conversation.

Much to my surprise and delight, my grandmother had also thought about what topics of conversation would be beyond southern gush and had pulled out some of her old scrapbooks with plenty of interesting black and white photographs from her childhood. My grandmother initiated a slightly more risky but fascinating conversation with Megan about what it was like to be 12 years old when she was growing up, while occasionally asking her great-granddaughter if this was similar to or different from her own experience. Megan came alive with interest and together they found mutual ground for a rich and rewarding conversation. We could have spent the evening talking about diet or health or school subjects or the extreme heat wave that we were experiencing, but fortunately we did not. The time passed quickly. Over the 83-year span they connected! We were all richer from the experience.

Communication Is a Two-Way Street

A large part of good communication is being a good listener. Megan had to listen to her great-grandmother and vice versa. Think about this: God gave us two ears and one mouth, so perhaps this means we should listen twice as much as we talk! Listening is a crucial skill in the art of conversation, and nowhere is it more needed than when trying to talk seriously to those in our extended families, especially across the generations.

One problem with listening is that we can listen more quickly than others can talk, so we have to listen intentionally—not just think about what we want to say when the other person stops talking. Everyone desires to be really heard. And most people—regardless of how shy they seem—do enjoy talking about themselves and think that they have something of value to share in a conversation. You can communicate the fact that you value the opinion of others by asking open-ended questions and listening to what they have to say. Please refer to the sidebar on the next page for some suggested open-ended questions you might try out the next time you are with your family.

Communicating Across the Miles

We often hear others complain about how it's not fair that their children and grandchildren live so far away. It's true that many extended families are scattered around the world, but it's not impossible to build long-distance relationships. We certainly have more ways to communicate than we did years ago; we simply need to use them. Fortunately, e-mail, newsletters, phones,

Open-ended discussion starters

Children
- What do you want to be when you grow up? Why?
- What is your favorite food? Why?
- What do you think God looks like?

Teenagers
- Who is your favorite/worst teacher or subject?
- Can you tell me about your best friend?
- What is your greatest hope/fear?

Young adults
- Who would your consider your hero or role model? Why?
- What is your favorite book/movie/music video? Tell me about it.
- Where do you see yourself in five years? Ten years?

Young married
- How did you meet? (Tell me about your first date.)
- How/when did you decide to get married? (Tell me about your wedding.)
- What was the most significant lesson you learned in your first year of marriage?

Parents
- How do you find time for yourself? (What gives you peace?)
- Tell me what a typical week is like at your house.

Empty nesters
- What do you do with your free time? (Hobbies)
- What do you want to do when you retire?

Grandparents
- Tell me about your grandchildren.
- What do you consider to be your greatest achievement?

Great-grandparents
- What has been the greatest change (social/technological/spiritual) in your lifetime?
- What wisdom do you have to pass along?

and instant messaging on the Internet can help to keep long-distance relationships close.

Some extended families have one interpreter who functions much like the old town crier. But try not to settle for secondhand news—always try to get it from the source. Many extended-family misunderstandings have arisen when information is told and retold, and then retold again. Just as in the game of "telephone," the information that starts through the round of players is almost never what the last person hears.

Our best source of tips for staying close across the miles is our survey participants who are doing it. Here's what some clever extended-family members wrote:

- "We call each other at halftimes or during sporting events on TV that we know we're interested in and are all probably watching. I'll call my brother-in-law and say 'Did you see that? Can you believe he blocked that goal? Okay, bye.'"
- "I read a book onto a cassette for my granddaughter, and then I mail both the book and tape to her. She loves it when a special 'grandma' package arrives."
- "I started an e-mail relationship with my grandson and have found that an e-mail conversation can go on and on. Our e-mails can be short or long, but they really help us connect with each other."
- "I was struggling with my relationship with my mother-in-law. We seemed to have nothing in common, so I started e-mailing her and asking her questions about my husband's childhood. She really seemed glad I was interested and would e-mail me back with some great stories. Then I got brave enough to begin to ask her about her childhood. It was amazing. The last time we got together, she really seemed to like me!"
- "We gave my parents a fax machine for Christmas. Now we can fax recipes, quick notes, articles of interest, and so on. The kids fax their artwork and even some of their school papers. It's been a great way to stay in touch and share some of our daily life with them."
- "We send photos over the computer using a scanner or digital camera. Our family loves it and has started sending photos back to us as well."
- "We finally got brave enough to try video-conferencing software—you can talk face-to-face! It's an amazing technology!"

- "We started an extended-family Web site. Cousins have their own page and talk to each other through instant messaging. Other family members post pictures. We also have a family calendar where we can let the other family members know our schedule. This is really practical when we're on vacation or out of town—we include emergency contact numbers, which fortunately we haven't needed, but it's a good feeling to know that if needed, we can get in touch with one another quickly."

I Just Called to Say I Love You

The telephone can be both a blessing and a curse! Don't you hate those telemarketing calls when you're just sitting down to dinner? On the other hand, good news from extended family often comes first over the telephone.

For a number of years when we (Dave and Claudia) lived in Europe, the telephone was our link with parents and in-laws in the States. At that time it cost several dollars a minute to call to Europe, but little was as thrilling as hearing from family—except when the call came in the middle of the night.

My (Claudia's) father was "Mr. Frugal," but he loved talking to us and would splurge from time to time on transatlantic phone calls. Sometimes he got a baby-sitter on the line instead of us, which greatly displeased him. His solution? To call at 3 A.M. (European time) when the U.S. rates were low and he knew we would be home. The problem was that by the time I really awoke, the conversation was over and I couldn't remember what had been said. Then I couldn't get back to sleep and was a grouch the rest of the day. We can laugh about it today, but sadly most of those calls were counterproductive. If you're going to call your extended family, do it when the party who answers will be pleased!

One key we have found is to watch how frequently we call. If we are the only ones initiating the calls, we are probably calling too often. Also, we try to be sensitive to their schedules. Obviously, middle-of-the-night calls are out. Other inappropriate times to call are during the evening news, during mealtime, and early in the morning when parents are trying to get children off to school or relatives are walking out the door on their way to work.

Also, we try to be sensitive when family calls us. The minutes are piling up on their phone bill instead of ours. In the past, we offered to call them back and make our own contribution to the phone company. Now we have a family toll-free number so they can call on our bucks.

If you would like to have deeper and richer conversations with your extended family, such conversations can and will take place if you are willing to be proactive and look for ways to connect. Also, you need to learn how to speak the truth in love. Even though risk is involved, if you craft your conversations and respect proper boundaries, your rewards can be great.

Speaking the Truth in Love

Sometimes when we are with extended family, our only choice *appears to be* peace versus honesty or truth versus polite civility. We believe this is a false dichotomy and implies wrongly that honesty is always hard and painful or that peace is always a cover for the truth. This way of thinking is unacceptable. Instead, what is needed is to learn "to speak the truth in love." This is the advice that the apostle Paul gave the church in Ephesus. Paul claimed that by learning to speak the truth in love, the Ephesians would build up the whole body of the church into maturity (Ephesians 4:15).

Exactly the same thing applies to extended families—as we learn to speak the truth in love, we will all be built up together, having the things that make for corporate growth and maturity. In learning to speak the truth in love, we will also learn to be honest and truthful while maintaining peace and love. Both are necessary, for honesty and truth can be used as a weapon to hurt or maim other family members if peace and love are not present. The reverse is not helpful either: Peace and love are meaningless if honesty and truth are not present.

Ways to Use the Phone in a Positive Way
- If you get their answering machine, leave a brief message or hang up before the beep.
- Use your own answering machine when you don't want to be disturbed.
- Vary the times you call. Be unpredictable. Unless your family prefers it, don't make it a ritual like the mother-in-law who for 30 years called every Sunday evening at 7 p.m.
- When you have nothing else to say, hang up—in a nice way, of course.

Take the Risk

Learning to speak the truth in love requires practice and patience and involves some risk. Only through taking risks do we discover rich and rewarding relationships. Expert investors on Wall Street tell us that without risk there is no reward, and athletic trainers say, "No pain, no gain!" Someone in the family needs to take the risky lead to move an extended family beyond chitchat—prayerfully, that person might just be you!

The late Rev. Dr. Dale Milligan, who founded the youth ministry Logos Systems Associates, formerly Youth Club, more than 40 years ago, was fond of the following story:

Dr. Milligan came home one day from work, a briefcase in one hand and a load of papers and books in the other. As he entered the front door, he saw his young daughter perched on the stairs directly in front of him. When she saw him, she impulsively jumped in his direction, obviously expecting her father to catch her as she flew through the air. Of course, he dropped everything in his arms and caught her.

Dr. Milligan claimed that this is an excellent illustration of how rich relationships properly develop, because, he would explain, healthy relationships require *risk, trust, vulnerability,* and *commitment.* His daughter took some *risk* by jumping into the air. She made the leap because she *trusted* her father to catch her. Once airborne, she became *vulnerable* to injury. She could have fallen to the ground and gotten hurt, she could have missed her mark, she could have knocked him down, or they both could have ended up on the floor injured. But once she left that step and flung herself into the air, she made a *commitment* from which there was no return. Once she jumped, she had to follow through.

Risk, trust, vulnerability, commitment ... are all necessary to move beyond chitchat and into the arena of rich, honest, loving extended-family

---

Remember that your in-laws don't know all your family history, so be sure to fill them in on key details. Telling them stories of your growing-up years helps them feel included. Also, asking questions about your in-laws' childhoods will help you better understand them.

relationships. Will you be the one who will take that risky leap into the uncharted waters of conversation? Will you be the one to trust others? Will you be the one to make yourself vulnerable? And will you be the one who will exhibit the commitment to the extended family to make it happen? We hope so! The following suggestions will help you take the risk and speak the truth in love:

Talk about the ones you are with at that particular moment. This may be the most important tip in this section! We have heard from families who become frustrated when much of a family gathering is spent talking about people and relatives who are *not* even present. For example, much of the conversation at a gathering might be about the son who is a young naval officer on a boat in the Pacific Ocean or about a family living across the country who could not afford to attend the gathering.

While it is natural to talk about those missing, it's not necessarily helpful. It is natural to want to share family news, but it should be kept to a minimum. Excessive talk about absent family members leaves little opportunity for those present to move beyond small talk. Talking about others who are absent doesn't do much to enrich extended family relationships in lasting ways. We suggest that you take some time early in the visit to review family news but quickly move on and spend the bulk of your time speaking about the people who are present.

Communicate directly. We live in what is often called "the information age," but it has not been called "the *accurate* information age." Myths and urban legends thrive on the Internet. Journalistic integrity has been questioned. The tabloids thrive! And the op-ed page is more interesting to some

---

You may be surprised at some of the insights that age and experience afford the older generation. There are also times when you may have spent so much time with an issue or decision that asking advice from your parents or grandparents may provide that fresh or unobstructed view of the issue, or their response may clear the way for your "out of the box" thinking to kick in and find a resolution.

—JOHN AND MARGARET

than the news. The days of "just give me the facts, ma'am" seem to be over. Culturally speaking, we crave gossip and spin! Successful, healthy extended-family relations, however, require accurate information.

Don't fall into the trap of having one family member communicate most of the family news to all parties. This puts undue pressure on one person and leaves far too much room for editorial bias. As far as possible, share the responsibilities of communication broadly. Involving more people in the communication loop may not make the family news any more accurate, but doing so will give more people a chance to register their concerns.

Be aware of the total message. Remember that your body posture can communicate positive or negative thoughts and feelings. Most of us are well aware that we communicate with each other in ways beyond words. A number of years ago, Kodak did a study to determine what makes up the total message. These are the results:

1. Tone of voice accounts for 38 percent of the total message. Facial expressions and voice inflections can totally change the meaning of our words. The pace of our words or the tone that we choose also provides a clue about our level of excitement or wonder.

2. Body language accounts for 55 percent of the total message. The slightest grin suggests that a speaker found something to be humorous or cute. Our body language communicates volumes and is actually the majority of the message! A person who chooses to lie down with his eyes closed faces a credibility crisis when he says that he is listening closely. Conversely, choosing to pull your chair in close to the conversation, leaning forward and looking your extended family members in their eyes says, "I care."

3. The words that we speak make up only 7 percent of the total message. The next time you talk to family members, be aware that your words are only a small part of what you communicate.

Avoid giving unsolicited advice. We all know folks who seem to know it all and don't mind sharing their infinite wisdom with everyone in order to make all lives brighter. They often have good intentions and may even have great wisdom to share, but advice is usually not what people seek when communicating with extended family. In reality, most people make the best decisions they can given their own circumstances and tend to resent unsolicited advice. The key word here is *unsolicited.*

You may encounter family members who are in distress and do genuinely want the help and advice of those whom they trust and love. If advice is solicited, then give it—sparingly! We realize this is much harder to put into practice than to understand. But think for a moment: Many of us are easily offended when we receive unsolicited advice, yet we fail to understand why

---

One of the most difficult lessons we have had to learn in dealing with extended family is this: Keep some things to yourself—not everything you think of saying needs to be said! Both of us tend to be very open with each other and we just assume that it's okay to comment and give our opinion on just about everything. But when it comes to extended-family relationships, we have found that the more left unsaid, the better. If you asked our adult kids and their mates, they would probably tell you that it is a lesson we are in the process of learning, and I emphasize "process."

Jan says that she especially has had to learn this lesson the hard way. "I notice too many things and sometimes I think it would be better if I could shut out things a little more easily and just become oblivious to what is going on when I am with family. Sometimes my noticing everything is a good thing. When I see that one of my daughters-in-law just got a haircut, or is wearing a new outfit, I comment on it. But the flip side of being observant is painful for me—and my extended family. If I see that one of the grandchildren needs better nutrition or some different kind of disciplining—I am apt to "subtly" comment on that, too, or give "helpful" advice.

It's these "helpful" ideas that usually get either of us into trouble. We tend to think in terms of how we can be helpful when our helping is the very thing that probably causes the most irritation in our extended-family relationships. We want to "help," and typically our kids do not want our help. "That's hard to get into my head!" Jan says. So our goal is to become gentle, cautious advisers. We find that other parents we talk to also struggle with what to say and when to say it. Sometimes we think that if we form our advice as a question, it will not be noticed. We "innocently" push for control by asking questions, thinking that it is really not giving a message. Little do we know that our questions might as well be blatant suggestions for our family members to change. So we have to tell ourselves daily, be cautious with "help."

—DAVID AND JAN STOOP

others do not value our unsolicited advice. The parable of the log and the splinter from the Gospel of Matthew comes to mind here. Make sure the log is out of your own eye before you offer to help members of your extended family remove the splinter from their eyes.

Deal directly with contentious subjects. While at times the best path may be to avoid contentious subjects, there is a time and proper place for dealing with them. In the next challenge we'll look at how to remain civil and calm when you disagree. In the meantime, the following will help you bring the more difficult subjects out into the open when necessary and to discuss them productively, yet with as few hurt feelings as possible. Often, it's all in how you phrase what you want to say and how to avoid making attacking statements.

Use "I" statements; avoid "you" statements and "why" questions. Try to begin significant statements with "I" instead of "you." The effect is almost magical! The conversation begins to sound less adversarial, and those in dialogue move to a deeper level of communication—from facts to feelings. When you're about to use a "you" statement or "why" question, try rephrasing it. Consider the following examples:

• *You're discussing where to spend Christmas this year.* Instead of saying, "Why do you always insist we come to you? You know we'd also like to have Christmas in our home from time to time!" try, "I know how much it means to you to have us all come to you for Christmas, but this year we really want to celebrate the holidays in our own home. Would you consider visiting us this year?"

• *You're frustrated because your daughter is not taking her son (your grandson Carter) to church.* Instead of saying, "You never take Carter to church. You're setting a bad example. You should do better. You were raised differently," try, "I'm concerned that Carter rarely attends church. I worry that he will not develop the faith he'll need to help him overcome the obstacles he'll face in life. I know the church isn't perfect, but I believe by participating in a faith community he will find 'positive peer pressure' that will help him be strong and stand up for good."

• *You're trying to let your parents know that they are flooding your children with too many gifts.* Instead of saying, "You always spoil our children. Why do you continue to give them such expensive and lavish gifts when you know we can't compete with you?" try, "I'm concerned that our children have too many toys. Do you think you could cut back a bit on the gift giving? I don't want the children to come to expect gifts when you come to visit us."

• *Your daughter rarely calls to just say hello; she only seems to call when she wants something—like a loan!* Instead of saying, "Why can't you ever call just to say hello to me? You only call me when you want something and I'm sick and tired of being ignored," try, "I've really missed hearing from you lately. Why don't we set up a time each week (or month) when we can touch base by phone? When I don't hear from you for long periods of time, I feel out of touch with your life."

Let us remind you that when you talk with family, don't judge feelings. Feelings are neither right nor wrong. No one should argue with your feelings, nor should you argue with theirs—our feelings are our feelings. *Our* perception is, in fact, *our* reality, but our perception might not be right. By sharing our perception of reality, we begin to learn from each other and grow together. Our differences can then begin to bring us together rather than divide us.

As best you can, maintain a sense of humor. Maintaining a sense of humor is key to building successful extended-family relationships. Mark Twain wrote that humankind "in its poverty, has unquestionably one really effective weapon—laughter…. Against the assault of laughter nothing can stand."

We (John and Margaret) fondly recall one family outing at a restaurant. At the outset of the evening one family member, who shall remain anonymous, was in bad form and seemed determined to spoil the evening for everyone. At one point, someone asked if anyone had learned any new jokes. Miraculously and rapidly, the evening quickly changed. Soon, everybody was telling jokes and laughing hard. Our laughter was apparently contagious because strangers at nearby tables, as well as our waitress, entered into the fun. Who would have thought that simple joke-telling and heartfelt laughter could turn an entire evening around for one family with such surprising ease and grace—not to mention a whole section of a restaurant! Humor is important.

One way to speak the truth in love is to prepare ahead for potentially difficult conversations. We suggest making a list of topics that you find hard to talk about with your relatives. Then write your own "Instead of Saying" and "Try" statements. A little forethought will help you to be positive and loving as you use the helpful communication skills we've suggested.

Don't take yourself (or your work) too seriously. Not taking yourself too seriously goes deeper than just being able to laugh. It has to do with who we are in relation to other family members: You (or anyone else in your family) may be a very important person in the eyes of the world or you may have a very important job, but when you gather as family, you are just a member of the family, equally valued and equally loved—not for what you do in the world, but for who you are.

Family members who elevate themselves above others in the family make gatherings difficult on everyone. The good news is that God made us all unique—with different gifts, interests, and abilities. By not taking ourselves too seriously we show respect, love, and admiration for the others who are in our midst. Not taking ourselves too seriously shows that we care.

When we (Dave and Claudia) get together with our extended family, no one cares about or is impressed by the number of books we've written or the scope of our marriage seminars. What's important is that we are fun, positive people to be around and that we play and interact with other family members—in particular with our grandchildren. We've found that a direct track to relating to our sons and daughters-in-law is to pay attention to our grandchildren.

Look for times when life situations give you the opportunity for deeper connections. In our extended-family survey, when we asked, "What pulls you together as a family?" the top answer we received was "funerals and family crises." Consider your own experiences. Have you recently attended an extended-family funeral? If so, you probably have experienced some deep, rich conversations and felt a close connection with family.

The View from the Pulpit

As a pastor, I (John) observe that although funeral gatherings are sad occasions, surprisingly they often have very positive effects on extended-family relationships. I am always amazed at how frequently I overhear one family member say to another following a funeral, "We should get together more often. Why do we always wait for a funeral to get everybody together?" For some reason, the death of a loved one seems to move most people beyond chitchat and into important moments with other family members.

In some way, memories are actually relived and can rejuvenate us, reminding us of that which is good about our family. Career plans, dreams, and hopes for the future are often discussed. Extended-family funeral gatherings unwittingly teach us "to number our days" in a good way, reminding us that life is too short and too precious to waste on unimportant idle activity. People often return from funerals determined to work harder to do only important things, and they often leave the gathering determined to do better and try harder to stay in touch with members of their extended family. Too often we simply return to our lives and our old routines and forget the richer, deeper moments of conversation we experienced with our extended family at such gatherings. But we believe that the very serious challenge is to follow through on doing better and trying harder to stay in touch.

One mom told us how several years ago at her mother's funeral she was inspired to instigate a yearly extended family reunion. The first year she made family history books with a genealogy chart so grandchildren could understand and appreciate their own family history. Their family reunion is set each year on the day before her mother's birthday and last year included more than 60 people! This lady is a great example of following through on staying connected to extended family.

Laughter is actually good for your health. It dispels tension, lowers your blood pressure, and may even improve your outlook on life. Here are a few ways to lighten things up with your family:

- Inject humor into tense situations. Once Claudia sent a card that showed a bear walking across a stage. It said, "Please bear with me. It's just a stage I'm going through!" You may want to visit a card shop and keep a supply of humorous cards.
- Laugh together. Be willing to tell stories about silly things you did.
- Send humorous articles, cartoons, and other funny things of special interest.
- Pull out the old scrapbooks. We made a scrapbook of all the things that were on our refrigerator as our boys were growing up. That's always good for a laugh or two.
- Buy a good joke book.

A Family Mountain-Top Experience

In the last 13 years we (Dave and Claudia) have attended funerals for all four of our parents. Each funeral, though sad, was a precious time of pulling together as an extended family. Family and friends provided a smorgasbord of delicious food that always seemed to ease communicating and connecting on a deeper level, but one memory stands out among the rest. This was when Claudia's father passed away 13 years ago. Our children came from near and far to be with us and to say good-bye to a grand old man.

After attending the funeral service and spending time with our many extended-family relatives, our sons asked us to slip away with them. They took us to the top of Talona Mountain, located at the beginning of the Blue Ridge Mountains just south of Ellijay, Georgia. Years ago on this spot, Claudia's father built a tall cross that is lighted at night and can be seen for miles and miles. Many are the stories of those passing through Ellijay and seeing the cross who were encouraged, comforted, or actually had a life-changing encounter with Jesus Christ. On this occasion the cross encouraged and comforted us.

Standing by the cross that evening, each of us shared a special memory of Joel Stembridge, father, grandfather, father-in-law, grandfather-in-law, and friend to all of us. We laughed as we remembered how he made fruitcakes every Christmas without a recipe and how he tried to tune the piano. He was convinced he could do anything!

We humbly acknowledged his sacrificial life and how he went the extra mile to help others discover a living and vital faith in God. We talked about his contagious laugh and how he asked one of our sons, "When are you going to marry this charming girl you've just introduced me to?" (Actually, they married six months later!) Through our laughter and tears we honored a great man, father, grandfather, and extended family member who would be sorely missed but never forgotten. Years later, his influence on our lives continues.

What life situations are you presently facing that offer a unique opportunity to connect with your loved ones? Use the hard times as opportunities to reach out and touch each other. And let that deeper connection enhance your communication in the ebb and flow of life. Daily, you can move beyond chitchat and speak the truth in love.

Remember: Life Is Short; Life Is Long

Life is short, but also life is long. Not every moment is a teachable moment. Not every conversation will be a connecting and meaningful one. There is a time and a season for every matter under heaven. Although we all crave deeper patterns of communication with our extended families, there are times that are just too testy to risk such moments. On those occasions, chitchat is enough. Not every family gathering, not every reunion, not every phone call or letter needs to be about the deeper issues of life. We are all at different points on our journey, so we encourage you to remember that life has many seasons. Enjoy them all!

Being Civil, Calm, and Clear When You Disagree

When the Scott siblings get together, they tend to revert to ancient established sibling pecking orders. For instance, Jan and her younger brother, Sean, pick up where they left off in junior high. Jan still sees Sean as the 13-year-old who bugged her continually. Sean still casts Jan in the role of the irritating older sister who embarrasses him around his friends. Add junior high humor to this and watch out! This humor can regress to a juvenile level of cutting and sarcastic remarks.

Can you identify with Jan or Sean? Or have you ever had the experience of going home to visit your parents and instead of civil and clear communication, conflict from the past reappeared? For example, the serious, thoughtful person falls back into being the family clown. The family rebel, long since settled into life with a wife and three kids, finds himself arguing like an angry teenager with siblings and parents. The responsible, competent career woman becomes an irresponsible daughter, and the parents turn into The Parents again.

In the classic movie *On Golden Pond,* daughter Chelsea visits her parents with her fiancé and 13-year-old soon-to-be-adopted son. Suddenly she finds herself back in the middle of conflict with her father, Norman. To her mother

Chelsea says, "I'm in charge in L.A., but I come here and feel like a fat little girl." Even though she thrives, is in control, and acts civil in all other environments, in the presence of her parents she once again becomes a little girl and conflict erupts. Can you identify with her?

Old hurts surface from the past and keep Chelsea and Norman from communicating in a clear, calm, and civil way. Her mom's good advice to her daughter is, "You have a big chip on your shoulder that is very unattractive. Everyone looks back on their childhood with some regret. Life marches on. Chelsea, I suggest you get on with it."

Later, as Chelsea is trying to process and to move past her anger with her dad, she asks her mother, "Why wasn't he my friend? Why can't he be my friend?"

Her mother replies, "Norman is 80 years old and has heart palpitations. When do you expect this friendship to begin?"

Both Norman and Chelsea need to let go of the past and try a little civility, to drop their unrealistic expectations. Communicating clearly and civilly when you don't see eye-to-eye is not easy for Chelsea and Norman, nor is it for any extended family member. Sometimes lack of common interests adds to the distance in relationships, as do long silences and lack of communication. When conflict exists, sometimes parents, adult children, and siblings choose peace as more desirable than open conflict.

What about others in your extended family? What roles do they play? Does one family member always seem to pick a fight? Is this just part of being in an extended family?

According to our survey, the answer may be yes—anger and conflict thrive in the extended family. Issues that create anger and conflict are often ignored, however. One of the most common answers we received to the question, "How do you resolve conflict in your extended family?" was "We don't," or "We just ignore it." But the good news is you can take some positive steps to beat this challenge of dealing with anger and conflict. Start by being civil, calm, and clear when you disagree.

BE CIVIL

It's important to realize that the goal is to build positive relationships with our extended family members, not tear them down. But unlike in the nuclear family, we have fewer opportunities to interact and connect with extended family members. So when extended families do get together, how can we resist reverting to childhood roles where Mom and Dad resume their parental roles?

Chelsea's mom discovered that letting go of young adult children is not an easy task. In *Families at the Crossroads,* author Rodney Clapp writes, "Truly letting a child go is hard, not only because of the pain of separation, but because a child fully released will reclaim and reshape the relationship in a way that may not be entirely to the parents' liking."[1]

Just as parents must release their children and reconnect with them as adults, adult children must release unrealistic expectations they have concerning their parents. Chelsea needs to come to the understanding that she and Norman can be civil to each other, but they probably will never have a close friendship.

Civility Tips for Relating to Parents:
• Assure your parents of your love, even if you don't see eye-to-eye with them.
• Realize you are not going to change your parents.
• Be interested in their lives.
• Move on with your life!

Civility Tips for Relating to Adult Children:
• Accept that they are adults.
• Accept who they are.
• Give up trying to control them.
• Adore their children (your grandchildren).

Civility Tips for Relating to Siblings:
• Check your humor!
• Stay in touch.
• Look for common interests.
• Appreciate the nieces and nephews.

Civility Tips for Relating to Single Adults:
• Be sure to include them in family activities.

- Be interested in their lives.
- Don't bug them about getting married.
- Get to know their friends.
- Phone often just to say hello.

Being Civil with In-Laws

In-law relationships also need a touch of civility. Stephanie complained, "My mother-in-law never approves of the way I do anything. The last time Joe and I visited her, it happened again. Just trying to be nice and helpful, I washed all the pots and pans after dinner. No sooner had I finished than she washed them all over again!"

Stephanie is not a newlywed. She has been married to Joe for 15 years. That whole time, she and Joe's mom have silently struggled with being civil to each other. When Joe's mom comes to visit, Stephanie really tries to get the house clean and comfortable for her. But after arriving, her mother-in-law pulls out the cleaning supplies and spit shines the bathrooms and kitchen. Stephanie assumes she's doing this because she thinks Stephanie is a slob and lives in filth.

After the last pots-and-pans fiasco, Stephanie spilled her frustrations to Joe's older sister, Connie. "I know your mother hates me and thinks I'm a slob and a bad person. I can't seem to do anything to please her."

Connie replied, "Stephanie, it's not about you. It's about Mom's com-

---

The ABCs of Family Civility

- Smile. People respond better to those who are positive.
- Be considerate. Ask yourself, "Is what I am about to say going to encourage and build up the other person, or tear him or her down?"
- Practice restraint and don't yell or raise your voice.
- Give sincere praise.
- Have the courage to admit it when you are wrong.
- Avoid ridicule and don't humiliate or demean the other person. You can express your anger without attacking the other person.
- Accept kindness from others and let others be nice to you.[2]

pulsion to have everything spotless. I grew up with her. I know her. She was like this before you and Joe even met. When she rewashes the pots and pans, it's not condemning you—it's simply that she has different (and what most would consider absurd) standards of what is acceptably clean. Let it go. There are bigger hills to die on."

While Stephanie couldn't really forget it and totally let it go, she did begin to look at her mother-in-law in a different light. She tried to find ways to help that didn't involve meeting her mother-in-law's high standard of cleanliness—like running to the grocery store for milk or dropping off the dry cleaning and laundry. Stephanie will probably never have a close relationship with her mother-in-law, but these days they are much more civil to each other.

Civility Tips for Relating to In-Laws:
• Be proactive. Do what you can to build the relationship.
• Don't compete with other family members.
• Refocus your perspective by looking for the positive.
• Accept reality.

As you keep civility a high priority in your extended family relationships, it becomes easier to focus on another effective way of dealing with anger and frustration—remaining calm. What 1 Corinthians 13 says about love can also be true for civility. This really works: Try reading the love passage substituting the word *civility* or *civil* for the word *love*. If you can succeed in remaining civil, you also up your chances of remaining calm even when you are so upset you could spit nails.

BE CALM

In a marriage or in a nuclear family, it's easier to manage conflict and anger than in the extended family. You're together and relate to each other every day. You have made a commitment to one another to work things out, and you have the time and opportunity to process your anger and find resolution. In the extended family, managing conflict and anger is much more complicated. The ones creating the anger and conflict may be halfway across the country. The conflict can be multifaceted and include numerous family members who each see a different facet of the conflict. How can you remain calm? Start by dealing with your own emotions.

In Your Anger Do Not Sin

The time to be calm and deal with your own feelings is when you are starting to react with anger. The Bible tells us, "In your anger do not sin" (Ephesians 4:26). That is quite a challenge in the extended family! This verse also tells us, "Do not let the sun go down while you are still angry." Is it possible to live out these admonishments?

Yes, but first we need to understand that anger is a God-given emotion, and we need to learn how to manage and process it in a godly way that builds our family relationships instead of tearing them down. Anger is actually a secondary reaction to fear, frustration, or hurt. When Stephanie's mother-in-law rewashed the pots and pans, Stephanie became angry. Why? Perhaps she was frustrated that she couldn't please her mother-in-law or felt hurt and rejected. That hurt, rejection, or frustration quickly turned to anger. Let's consider another family where civility and calmness were needed.

Three Sons and a Dad

Kevin and his two older brothers grew up in the family business. Their dad was a printer and had built his printing business into a successful enter-

---

Eight Ways to Calm Down

- Try counting to 10.
- Take a walk or go for a jog.
- Get some space. Run an errand or go to your room for a while.
- Read a passage of Scripture prayerfully and repetitively (e.g., Psalm 94:18-19; Psalm 103; Lamentations 3: 19-33).
- Journal your feelings.
- Pour out your soul to God in prayer, expressing everything—even anger.
- Talk to a close confidant, counselor, or friend.
- Sing an old spiritual or hymn ("Nobody knows the trouble I've seen....").

prise. Growing up, all three sons worked in the business, but Kevin was the only one to remain in town to help his dad with the company. He actually turned down a great opportunity to get in on the ground floor of an international energy conglomerate. It would have required traveling all over Europe, however, so he decided to stay home and work with his dad, who needed him.

His two older brothers had already left home to pursue other careers. Nathan, the oldest brother, lived on the West Coast and went into telecommunications. He was so successful that in his late forties, he retired early. Brian, the middle son, was a professor at a small New England university.

Then their dad died, leaving his estate—including the printing business—equally to all three sons. Kevin was furious. He was the son who gave up his dreams and stayed home to help his dad run the business, and it just wasn't fair that he would now have to share the business with his two older brothers, who had financial security.

What about Brian and Nathan? They both thought that Kevin had been living off their dad and not doing his share of the work. As they began to execute the will, they discovered that Kevin had taken some financial liberties that he should not have taken—especially in the last year of their dad's life when he was not able to be involved in the day-to-day business of the print shop. Civil? Calm? Forget it! Angry? You bet!

Managing Your Anger

- Choose an Anger Motto. Repeat to yourself as often as necessary a phrase like: "I have a choice; I choose not to be angry."
- Keep an Anger Calendar. On a calendar mark the days when you really get angry. You may not be aware of how often you explode with anger.
- Identify Your Hot Buttons. If you track what makes you angry, you can think ahead of ways to defuse those situations.
- Rule Out Name-Calling. Don't label the other person as a jerk or something worse. It will be harder to feel empathy, which can help you diffuse anger.
- Face the Real Issue. Stop and identify what the real issue is and confront it in a polite but assertive way.[3]

Add to the mix more extended-family relationships—three sisters-in-law and grandchildren, including Kevin's son who was caught in the middle wanting to be loyal to his dad but really loving both uncles—and you have a full-blown extended family crisis with plenty of anger. How could they possibly "be angry and not sin"?

First we might point out that there is a difference between having feelings of anger and living out angry behavior. After angry words had been exchanged, the brothers needed to back up and process their own anger before trying to find a family solution. And that's the best place for any angry family member to start.

First Deal with Your Own Anger

When negative feelings arise, we need to first look inside before we can relate to those around us. Dr. Harriet Lerner, in *The Dance of Anger*, writes, "When emotional intensity is high, many of us engage in nonproductive efforts to change the other person, and in so doing, fail to exercise our power to clarify and change our own selves." She suggests the following questions to ask yourself when you are getting angry:

- What am I really angry about? [We would add: What am I fearful of? What is frustrating me? What am I hurt about?]
- What is the problem and whose problem is it?
- How can I sort out who is responsible for what?
- How can I learn to express my anger in a way that will not leave me feeling helpless and powerless?
- When I am angry, how can I clearly communicate my position without becoming defensive or attacking?
- What risks and losses might I face if I become clearer and more assertive?[4]

Remember, we can't change another person by direct action. When we begin to process our own anger in a civil and calm way, however, many times others may also calm down and be more civil in response to us. Dr. Lerner notes:

"We are responsible for our own behavior. But we are not responsible for other people's reactions; nor are they responsible for ours.... We begin to use our anger as a vehicle for change when we are able to share our reactions without holding the other person responsible for causing our feelings, and without blaming ourselves for the reactions that other people have in response to our choices and actions."[5]

When we are aware of our own negative feelings and their source, we can begin to calm down. And if you can remain civil and calm in the midst of a chaotic encounter with your extended family, perhaps you will have enough energy to focus on being clear. True communication is not an entirely unnatural phenomenon, but in our experience it is more of a rarity than most of us realize—especially when we are dealing with those beyond the walls of our homes.

BE CLEAR

Misunderstandings happen when we assume the other person knows how we feel and what we think, but with the extended family you can't be too clear! When John's parents were planning a visit, we (John and Margaret) came up with a great way to be clear.

We are in the stage of life that feels like the *Star Wars* scene when Han Solo says, "Fasten your seatbelts and prepare for light speed." John's parents—simply put—are not anywhere near the "light speed" stage, and recognizing this on the front end, we decided to try and come up with a helpful tool for them to step into our world and not have their heads spin. We hit

Getting Help from God

Since anger is a God-given emotion, we can look to Him for help in processing it. When you become aware that you are getting angry, acknowledge your anger to God and ask Him to help you deal with your negative feelings. Since anger is a secondary reaction, think about what is the primary source of your anger. Are you fearful? Frustrated? Hurt? Admit your feelings to God and pour out your heart in prayer to your heavenly Father. You may find it helpful to read Scripture aloud and pray it back to the Lord. We suggest starting with the following verses:

- Psalm 138:7-8
- Psalm 31
- Proverbs 13:12

on the idea of an itinerary for their visit, complete with meal times and places and even menus when we knew them.

By providing an itinerary, we gave them some idea about what to expect ahead of time. The results were that they felt more comfortable anticipating each day, giving them the opportunity to balance activities with rest time. A sense of humor is a prerequisite for the name Bell, so as we wrote the itinerary, we incorporated a great deal of what we consider a sense of fun. This meant including things like "lights out" and "attitude adjustment hour." At any rate, the visit was a smashing success according to everyone. So we encourage you to think outside the box for ways to make being with your extended family a pleasant experience for all.

But what about those times when you don't have a clear itinerary and you need to find some clarity? What can you do to address the situation and move on while being civil, calm, and clear? While you can't force others to address conflict, you don't have to ignore it. Ignoring conflict will not make it go away, and family relationships will not improve until communication is restored.

Dealing effectively with family conflicts might be compared to taking a trip and trying to chart your way on a map. If you miss a turn or make just one small turn in the wrong direction, you won't end up where you want to be.

Dave is an explorer at heart. Getting lost is just part of the adventure. Claudia likes to chart the course, and while she also likes a little adventure, she'd prefer not to experience it in the car. When we travel we know our roles. Dave drives, Claudia navigates. All is fine when she is reading the map accurately and when Dave follows directions. But sometimes he doesn't listen when Claudia announces an upcoming turn.

Recently, we had one such experience. The setting was in Kufstein, a small town in the Austrian Alps. Our assignment was to find a particular computer store to get help for our e-mail system that wasn't working. We could receive e-mails but not send them—talk about messed-up communication! But on this day our challenge was to find the computer store in the maze of narrow, one-way streets. To complicate our challenge, Kufstein is divided right down the middle by a river.

Dave, an avid tourist, was enthralled with the old buildings and cobblestone streets and didn't hear Claudia tell him to turn right. That one missed turn led us to the other side of the river. Dave absolutely hates to ever turn around, and he kept trying to get back to the other side of the river without retracing our way back over the major connecting bridge.

Claudia was disgusted. "Why don't you just turn around? Why didn't you listen to me when I said to turn right before the bridge?" We were both frustrated.

Do you ever feel as if you've made a wrong turn but you don't want to admit it? Maybe then it's time to stop, turn around, and listen to another person's advice. That's what Dave did; then it was simple to find the computer store.

The Art of Listening

The most important form of communication and conflict resolution is listening. We talked about its importance in the last challenge, but it's so important that we want to mention it again. Until we really concentrate on listening, our attempts at communicating and resolving conflict can be "dialogues of the deaf." Many times we are so preoccupied with the point we want to make that we don't really hear what the other is trying to say. If we can listen long enough to help identify the real problem, however, then possibly we can discuss it together in a civil, calm, and clear way.

Gloria Scott and her daughter Jan decided to plan an engagement party for Hayley and Bill. Gloria has in mind a more traditional engagement party that would include many if not most of her and Paul's friends. Jan is thinking more along the lines of hiring a DJ and creating a guest list composed of Hayley's friends. Since Gloria and Jan don't get to visit in person often, they are careful to try not to hurt each other's feelings. However, working together on a significant event in the life of their family when they are approaching it from two different viewpoints makes the going a little sticky.

Jan:	"I can call my friend Rachel and see if she knows which DJ we should try to line up."
Gloria:	"Oh don't do that—that is way too much trouble."
Jan:	"No, really, I don't mind."
Gloria:	"I can take care of the music. Don't worry about it."
Jan:	"Well, Rachel just had a huge surprise birthday party for her husband—I'm sure she won't mind if we use the same DJ, and

I think she had a friend just starting out in the catering business help with the food."

Gloria: "Now Jan, please, I insist! You don't want to spend all your time while you are home tracking down people and phone numbers. I can arrange the music and the food."

Jan: "It's just that I'm sure that everyone would really enjoy a party like the one for Rachel's husband."

Gloria: "I am not sure that your father's friends would be entirely comfortable with that DJ. I think a small ensemble might be more appropriate."

Jan: "Oh."

At this point Gloria and Jan are interrupted by children requesting a snack. Jan is silently fuming and pulls Steve aside and says, "I can't believe we are expected to help with a party for a bunch of old people—I thought this was supposed to be a party for Hayley and Bill!" Meanwhile, Gloria seeks solace from Paul by reporting, "I know Jan and Steve can't afford to host a party for Hayley and Bill on their own; I'm just trying to help create a really nice party and include people who will be invited to the wedding."

Gloria and Jan resume their conversation:

Jan: "Mom, I think Hayley and Bill would really have fun with their friends at this party if we get a DJ—not a hoity-toity string ensemble."

A good listener:

• Focuses on the speaker's message
• Doesn't defend himself or rebut the speaker
• Repeats what he hears for clarification
• Asks follow-up questions

Listening is not:

• Just waiting for your turn to speak
• Thinking about how you are going to respond
• Only keeping your mouth shut

Gloria: "Dear, our friends will be coming to the wedding and sending them lovely gifts, and they should be included in the engagement party. A DJ would just be way too noisy and loud for them."

Jan: "What I hear you saying is that this is really your and Dad's party and you are going to do it your way."

Gloria: "No, not at all—this is for Hayley and Bill; we just want it to be a really nice, elegant party."

Jan: "They don't want nice and elegant—they want fun."

At this point in the conversation, things can go from civil and calm to chaotic and critical. Although they have remained civil and calm to this point, they have not communicated clearly. Gloria needs to be more honest and direct, and Jan needs to take a less confrontational approach. Perhaps the conversation could continue like this:

Gloria: "Maybe we should revisit the whole party idea. I know in my day an engagement party was thrown by the bride's parents and included their friends. Maybe that's not the way things are done anymore."

Jan: "Well, it isn't that your friends shouldn't be invited. It just seems like the party is really for Hayley and Bill and should be more geared to their idea of a fun party."

Gloria: "Where can we reach a compromise here? I would really like to include our friends—I don't want their feelings to be hurt by not being invited."

Jan: "How about if we have food first and just have the DJ later—everyone would have the chance to visit, and if people didn't want to stay and dance or whatever, they could leave."

This is how the Scotts remained civil, calm, and clear while working through a potential conflict. Remember, the goal is to build positive relationships, to deal with your own emotions, and not to assume the other person knows how you feel and what you think. Actively and intentionally listening to the other person can make a tremendous difference in the outcome of the conversation.

Speak Clearly

Listening is vital, but you also need to be clear when you speak. Good communication occurs when you really want to connect with the other person. Be willing to say what you really mean, but craft your sentences so that you don't attack the other person. It may be helpful to remember to start your sentences with "I" and let the statement reflect back on you. No mind reading—you really don't know what the other person is thinking!

Gloria might have said to Jan, "I feel frustrated when we try to plan a party for Hayley and Bill, and my friends aren't being considered."

Jan might have said, "I want to include everyone, but I'm concerned that we're forgetting that this party is really in honor of Hayley and Bill."

These "I" statements foster understanding and would be much safer and more appropriate than saying, "You aren't considering my friends at all!" or "Why can't you see this is a party for Hayley and Bill, not for your friends?"

Look for the Positive

Along with speaking clearly, let us encourage you to look for the positive. You might want to track your ratio of positive to negative statements. To keep your conversations positive you need to make at least five positive statements for every negative statement. How are you doing? You might want to listen to yourself the next time you are together with family and mentally keep track of your positive and negative statements. Then remember five to one is just staying even. If the relationship is already stressful, you'll need to increase the ratio. Some psychologists suggest seven positives to one negative is better. To give you some positive ammunition, you might want to list the admirable qualities of the relative with whom you are struggling. For instance, regarding her mother-in-law, Samantha wrote: "She loves my husband; she prays for our family; she makes a great pumpkin pie. She remembers my birthday."[6]

PROBLEM SOLVING 101

Once you've managed to avoid a major family blowup, you can move on to trying to find workable solutions. Let's revisit the Scotts as they try to plan an extended-family vacation.

Planning a Beach Vacation

The Scott family is trying to plan a family get-together at the beach. The problem is everyone has different ideas about just how to do an extended-family vacation. Here's a sampling of some of the challenges and issues they are facing:

- Which beach to go to and what price of beach house to rent. Paul and Gloria want to go to Florida because that's where the family went each summer when their children were growing up. J. Paul Jr. and Julia want to go to the Outer Banks of North Carolina—it's more upscale and less crowded. Jan and Steve prefer coastal Georgia because it's cheaper and not such a long drive. Sean and Hayley really don't care.
- Whether to bring a baby-sitter so the adults could have time together.
- Who will be in charge of meals—planning, shopping, cleaning up.
- When and where will they go out for meals, and who will pay for what.
- What about Sean—if he can bring a friend, why can't the others?
- Other assorted issues dealing with sleeping arrangements—this will be a month before Hayley's wedding—and who will get the rooms with private baths.

Now let's see how the Scotts handle these issues. To identify the issues, they use the "who, what, when, and where" technique. Since the Scott grandchildren are old enough to have and voice their opinions, they also want to be included in the big family meeting.

Who? All of the Scotts agree that what they would really like is for the entire family to be together for at least one week of summer vacation. This answers the "who" question.

What? Vacation to Julia means not having to cook or clean up. Sean would prefer cooking while on vacation because he normally does not have the time to cook the way he enjoys cooking, nor does he have the opportunity to cook for a crowd because he is single. Jan knows her children are easy to please with meals and does not feel strongly about having to cook. Hayley doesn't cook—Bill does, but won't; besides, she will be one month away from her wedding and preoccupied with those plans anyway. It is eventually agreed by all that each family will bring whatever special provisions they require for breakfast and lunch each day, and each family will take a turn providing dinner in, out, or take-out during the vacation. One night will be free for all to make their own choices. This answers the "what" question.

When? Everyone pulls out his or her respective calendar. Miraculously they find one week the following summer between school and work schedules, volunteer commitments and charity events, various sports seasons, and Hayley's approaching wedding that everyone can make. Eureka! Next it is decided that they will rent the house for two weeks. The first week is the family-only week and the second week will accommodate the baby-sitter as well as any friends the grandchildren wish to invite. Jan and Steve bow out of the second week gracefully by claiming that time for their own family camping expedition. Hayley decides she might as well stay and even keep her soon-to-be stepchildren. Sean invites two friends to join him for the second week, and J. Paul Jr. and Julia decide to invite Julia's parents since Jan and Steve won't be staying. Paul and Gloria can't imagine not capitalizing on the opportunity to be with any of their family, and Paul chivalrously tells Gloria that she is welcome to join him on his daily, quiet fishing expeditions. This answers the "when" question.

Where? Paul thinks escaping in his flat-bottomed fishing boat for a few hours of solitude with a fishing pole in his hand defines the very idea of vacation. J. Paul Jr. cannot possibly envision any vacation that does not include 18 holes of golf per day (minimum), and Sean would not be able to tolerate the idea of an isolated, remote beach with no nightlife or singles activities available. Steve is mostly concerned with the financial aspect of any vacation and can imagine making do with a much less luxurious vacation setting to accomplish being together. In fact, he proposes camping as a viable alternative. The grandchildren cannot fathom a vacation without cable television and a Blockbuster store nearby, and Hayley thinks a fax machine will be necessary for last-minute wedding details.

The one thing everyone does agree on from the first is that this year it must be a beach vacation. Beyond that, it must have an inland waterway for fishing, several golf courses nearby, nightlife options within a reasonable drive, and affordable rentals available. They have found common ground— which is not easy—and Gloria calls her travel agent for help finding a large rental house that can accommodate all of them and which divided equally (another decision everyone agreed on) will not place too much of a financial burden on anyone. Everyone also agrees that equally divided, the rental costs must not exceed a reasonable amount per family.

Gloria also carefully explains that cable television and a fax hookup are a must—as well as allowance for pets, since Steve wants to board their Lab. Julia heads for the bookstore to get the latest travel magazines and books on the beaches they have discussed, and Sean gets online to research the same beaches via the Internet. Fortunately for the Scotts, each source they sought suggests one of the South Carolina beaches. This answers the "where" question.

Another important point when working through issues is to determine whose problem it is and others' contributions to it. For the Scotts, each issue "belonged" to a different family member, and working through to a solution required everyone's patience and perseverance. Once the "who, what, when, and where" issues were resolved, it became easier to assure all that their concerns about certain issues were heard and acknowledged. For instance, Steve's financial concerns were dealt with in a dignified manner by setting a limit on the cost of the rental house and including the requirement for pets to be allowed. Paul and J. Paul Jr.'s requirements for an inland waterway and golf course accessibility were met, as was Sean's request for nearby nightlife options.

The Scotts met and solved their other challenges when they chose to rent for two weeks instead of one to accommodate the differing viewpoints on inclusion and exclusion of nonfamily members, including a baby-sitter. The meal issue was resolved by each family unit's having the responsibility and choice for one family meal duty each week. The rooms with private baths were to be divvied up one private bath per family, and each family could then choose how to best arrange themselves.

The Scotts, a composite of extended families across America, accurately reflect one of the most difficult truths of family clans—income levels may vary greatly from family to family. Thus, for some families within an extended family this requires careful and thoughtful planning—whether it is a vacation, birthday, anniversary, retirement, visit, or even meals together being planned. We (John and Margaret) know an extended family that struggles over European vacations and flying first class, as well as an extended family that struggles over whether to pay to reserve a campsite. The important thing for families to remember—no matter what their resource level— is that the goal is improving the relationship.

Family Brainstorming

As you talk about issues with your own extended family, it's important to isolate each issue and deal with them one by one. You'll want to brainstorm possible solutions. Be as creative as you can be and make a list. Remember, humor may help this process. Concentrating on a list of possibilities helped the Scotts stay focused on the issues. They stated the issues they felt strongly about when discussing this vacation and then methodically listed unanswered questions and concerns, marching through their list until each piece fell into place. Ultimately, this process was completed using the "who, what, when, and where" method, which allowed for a less emotional framework for discussions. Brainstorming is a great opportunity to be sure that everyone contributes at least one idea and voices an opinion in an unthreatening manner by simply going around the room and recording one solution per person.

Choose a Possible Solution and Try It

After you have brainstormed for a while, choose one possible solution and try it out. If it works, fine. If not, go back to your brainstorming list and try another. By extending the vacation to two weeks as an option, selecting a location to which everyone has access, agreeing on meal expectations, setting a limit for costs, and requesting certain parameters (i.e., golf courses, inland waterway, Blockbuster, cable TV, pets allowed, restaurants and nightlife nearby), the Scotts found a solution, and everyone felt a sense of ownership and excitement about the vacation. Don't forget that sometimes solutions require family members to compromise; certain expectations may need to be planned for a future get-together. Just be sure to follow through with those plans.

REMEMBER TO BE WILLING TO NEGOTIATE AND COMPROMISE

For the Scotts or any family to find a solution, they will need to be willing to negotiate and compromise. They will also need to realize their limitations. Following are some possible ground rules that will help you stay civil, calm, and clear when you disagree.

- *No name calling.* While at times it's tempting, it's not productive. Avoid it!
- *Stick to the issues.* The Scotts stuck to the issues. They could have become sidetracked by taking on Sean's relationship with his friend—

or hassling Hayley, who still plans to marry someone much older than she, someone who already has two kids.

- *Don't relive the past; stay in the present.* Bringing up the past is usually a one-way street to misunderstanding and anger.
- *Talk to the person with whom you are having the conflict.* A great general principle is to resist bringing other parties in on your conflict. Try to work it out between only those involved.
- *Finish your conversation.* Hayley dropped out of the deliberations before her issues were really addressed.
- *Show up happy.* In July when the Scotts get together, we hope that everyone seems content. Once you have worked through an issue, it's time to move on and try to put on a positive face.
- *Be a peacemaker.* Extended families are minefields for misunderstandings and conflicts. Keep your antennae up for ways you can be a peacemaker. You'll be a hero.

We called this challenge "Being civil, calm, and clear when you disagree." Notice we didn't say, "*if* you disagree." If you're family, from time to time you *will* disagree. But if you follow our suggestions, you will be able to work through your issues and find ways to compromise.

Promoting Harmony When You Get Together

As Gloria cleaned out the refrigerator after the Scott Thanksgiving get-together, she found the following evidence of their family's diversity and also a clue to why she was so exhausted:

- Five kinds of milk: One daughter drinks only organic milk; another, 2 percent milk. She also found nonfat, 1 percent, and whole milk for the younger children.
- Three kinds of orange juice: juice with no pulp, some pulp, and lots of pulp; and of course grape juice and apple juice—favorites of grandkids who don't drink orange juice!
- Four kinds of lettuce: Bibb, iceberg, romaine, and Boston.
- An assortment of vegetables, which reminded her of the vegetarians in the family, alongside five kinds of sandwich meats left by the family carnivores.

- Cheeses: Parmesan, cheddar, Swiss, provolone, American, and blue cheese—along with string cheese for the younger set.

If finding acceptable menus for the Scott family clan wasn't confusing enough, consider the diversity in personalities and lifestyles. Gloria wonders how adult children who grew up in the same home can have such different philosophies about parenting and life in general. She has grandkids on schedules and grandkids who set their own schedules. One family is quite structured while another family is free-spirited. How can kids that grow up in the same family be so different? Gloria doesn't understand what happened—they used to be so close and now they seem to be so disjointed. She wonders what she can do to get it back to the way they were.

Gloria's daughter Jan wonders why her mom can't just relax and accept that she is an adult and that the younger families are all different from the way their family was when she was growing up. Why does her mother try to act like an air traffic controller and tell everyone what to do or not do? She loves her parents, but she wants the freedom to be herself. Jan hates being over-scheduled and really wishes they could have just relaxed and enjoyed being all together. She also wishes her brother and sister-in-law would be a bit more flexible with their children. This isn't school—it's a time to kick back and enjoy one another.

Gloria and Jan represent different generations. Though their perspectives diverge, both would like for the whole family to get together without tension or being a catalyst for World War III. While we believe that's an entirely realistic and admirable vision, to promote harmony when the extended family gets together will require those on both sides of the generational seesaw to do a bit of adjusting.

Interestingly, many survey participants responded to the question, "What is the major tension in your extended family?" with the answer "Family get-togethers!" And to the question, "What are your favorite extended family traditions?" many others responded, "Family get-togethers." Family times together can be the best of times. They can also be the worst of times. How would you describe the last time your extended family got together? Tension-filled, or fantastic fun? Whatever your circumstances or past experiences may be, we believe you can make the most of your potential for successful family gatherings in the future.

In the following pages we will consider how to meet the challenge of promoting harmony when the whole family gets together. We'll consider what we can do to make family get-togethers work when we meet in neutral settings as well as in one another's homes. We'll look at holidays, traditions, and special occasions, as well as those times we get together because of a death or family crisis. Let's start with extended-family get-togethers.

EXTENDED FAMILY VACATIONS

In the last chapter the Scotts were hard at work planning for their extended-family vacation at the beach. They know that vacations can be glorious opportunities for quality extended-family time together. Unlike holidays or other special occasions, vacations are usually not fraught with high expectations or certain dyed-in-the-wool traditions for most extended families. This is partly because the dynamics of an extended family can change drastically from year to year, and thus vacation destinations and goals may differ dramatically. Considering the interests and preferences of all the members, discussing ahead of time who is in charge of planning, and deciding on financial responsibilities can ease a great deal of the turmoil sometimes associated with extended-family vacations.

Are We Having Fun Yet?

Some say that intergenerational family vacations are vacations from sanity. Yet families all across the country hit the roads together to experience their own brand of extended-family vacation. Packing three generations in a mountain cabin or rental beach house or campsite for one or two weeks can be daunting. Grown children may suddenly become teenagers again. Grandparents can unknowingly reassume the parental role and be much too "overprotective." And grandchildren can set one generation against the other—plus instigate their own civil wars among cousins. How can we keep the peace when we get together for vacations? Here are some tips:

- *Know your limits.* Think realistically about how long you want to be together. Personality differences, ages of children and grandparents, and closeness of relationships are all factors to be considered. We know one family that rents a house on the beach for two weeks each summer. Everyone is invited, but extended family members tend to come and go during those two weeks. The grandparents told us that four days is about right for them. They love their family but find eight grandkids, all under the age of seven, exhausting. By going for only part of the time, they don't wear out their welcome, and also it gives the middle and younger generations—siblings and families—time together to build their relationships.

- *Make a schedule.* When 10 or 15 people get together, it's great to have a plan. One family we know actually printed out an itinerary giving approximate times for meals, the beach, resting, crafts, and lights out. While it wasn't a hard-and-fast schedule, it helped to keep them on track. Kids knew that the hour after lunch was rest time (which the parents and grandparents needed!), and nagging about Play Station time was limited to the time allotted on the master schedule.

- *Share the load.* Decide up front who will have kitchen and KP duty and for which meals. It's easy to let grandmother or the most cooperative daughter/daughter-in-law become the kitchen help, but we've found that everyone can participate. Some of the best cooks in our families are the males!

- *Share the cost.* Depending on your family's financial situations, we suggest sharing the cost. Claudia's parents and a couple of tag-along aunts visited us in Vienna, Austria, and some of our best memories of their visits are the European vacations we took together. For each trip we had a financial kitty to which each person would contribute. We (Dave and Claudia) were exempted from "feeding the kitty," as we were the tour

Before the Vacation:

- Discuss your own nuclear family expectations for the get-together.
- Discuss ahead of time which "traditions" will be observed.
- Discuss who will be responsible for planning, paying, and/or hosting.
- Expect to compromise.
- Don't expect parents to continue to "do" for you (e.g., clean, cook, pay).
- Determine to be flexible.
- Include others in the planning.

guides and provided transportation. From the kitty we paid for hotels, food, and admission fees.

- *Take a break.* When the extended family is all together, we find we often need a breather. We (Dave and Claudia) can remember years ago slipping away with our boys from our extended family for milk shakes, and even now when we get together with our sons and their families we like to slip off for a private walk on the beach or hike up the mountain. We also look for one-on-one time with our grandkids. Recently, I (Claudia) had a great time making brownies with a grandson who was ready to come in from the beach before the others.

- *Take a swim.* Did you realize that swimming, or any physical activity, can help children calm down? And it also works for hyper adults! Physical exercise burns energy, so go swimming or take a hike or rent bikes. The point is, do something physical.

- *Include others.* One year our family took along two 13-year-old girls to help care for all the little kids in our family. They were charming girls and came prepared with creative crafts for the kids. Here's a tip: If you are experiencing some tension or strained relationships, including others can help keep a more positive atmosphere. Also, if you have young adolescents, they may be more fun to have around if they bring a friend.

- *Let the parents parent, and don't impose on the grandparents.* Know your boundaries and respect them. Need we say more?

Fun Activities for the Cousins

When everyone is together, be prepared with easy and fun activities for the younger children. Cousins might enjoy some of the following:

A fun extended-family vacation activity is to celebrate your own family uniqueness by designing family coats of arms. This can be done first with individual nuclear families and then as an entire extended family. (Trust us; grandparents will really enjoy this activity!) Be sure that each family member has the opportunity to contribute his or her ideas to the project. Your coat of arms can be designed to portray your family values, traditions, experiences, and goals.

- *Make a "You-Can-Eat-It" necklace.* Give each child a bowl of Cheerios and a bowl of Froot Loops (or any cereal with a hole in the middle) and a string. Let children create their own special necklaces. Then, with a glass of juice or milk, let them eat their necklaces. (Don't let them eat the string!)
- *Paint-by-water books.* Give each child a cup of water, a book, and a paintbrush. If you don't have paintbrushes handy, Q-tips work great and are a lot less messy than brushes.
- *Make Kool-Aid Play-Doh.* Mix together:
  2^1/2 cups flour
  ^{1}/2 cup salt
  2 packages unsweetened Kool-Aid
  Add:
  2 cups boiling water (An adult should add the water and supervise!)
  3 teaspoons cooking oil
  When cool enough, knead until smooth. Let the Play-Doh cool completely, and then have fun!
- *Make toothpick sculptures.* You will need toothpicks and marshmallows. Use the marshmallows to hold the toothpicks together as you build a sculpture.

FAMILY VISITS

When the family visits together at your house or theirs, the dynamics are different than meeting in a neutral location, and you will want to do what you can to make the get-together as pleasant as possible.

Plan Ahead for Family Visits

- Plan for a variety of activities during family visits.
- Explore new recreational, cultural, or educational opportunities.
- Plan from time to time to pick up the check when you go out together to a restaurant. Don't let your guests pay for everything!
- Invite others to share in the chores.

Recently, John's sister and family, who live in the Southeast, came to visit us in Colorado for a week. At first, the visit appeared to be doomed to a re-do of the old children's classic *Country Mouse, City Mouse.* However, in between our snowshoeing trek in waist-high snow with a picnic in subfreezing temperatures, meals together at home and at our favorite local haunts, and sharing several days skiing together, the cultural differences between their urban, Southeastern lifestyle and our Rocky Mountain outdoor lifestyle became far less significant than the joy we all experienced in the family memories we created together.

Whether you are visiting your parents or grandparents, they are visiting you, or you're getting together as siblings, a little forethought and planning can make a big difference in how successful the time together will be. Let's consider two major issues: Where will everyone sleep, and what will we eat?

Adequate Sleeping Arrangements

A key question for any family visit is, "Where will everyone sleep?" Recently we (Dave and Claudia) hosted all of our immediate extended family, which includes our three sons, three daughters-in-law, and seven grandchildren. Fifteen people in one condo can be very challenging and is extra hard if you're all tired and grouchy from lack of sleep. Few families have enough bedrooms or sleeping space to accommodate 15 people—we certainly don't—but here are some ideas we have used to provide adequate privacy and a comfortable place to sleep:

- Before family arrives, check the condition of your guest bed, hide-a-bed, futon, and so on. Sleep for one night on each. If you're not comfortable, family won't be either!
- Check your pillows. Old, musty pillows can keep family members awake and trigger allergies. We recently replaced our guest pillows with fresh ones for around 25 dollars.
- When buying a hide-a-bed, try it out before you buy it. Watch for bars under the mattress that can wreck your sleep as well as your back!
- Consider purchasing several three-inch-thick pieces of foam rubber. On the floor they can be quite comfortable. When not in use, you can roll them up or store them under another bed.
- We purchased kindergarten mats for our grandchildren. They love selecting their own mat and choosing where they want to sleep. (Of course, this is with their parents' approval!)

- Blow-up mattresses can be quite comfortable and are easy to store between visits.
- To deal with the politics of sleeping arrangements, come up with your own fair, consistent approach. For instance, the first to arrive or perhaps the longest visitor gets the best room.

Feeding the Family Clan

Whether at their house or yours, we suggest keeping your meals and entertaining simple. Here are some tips that help us simplify providing meals:

- Get others involved. Assign chores and make sure everyone has a job—bringing the dessert, fixing the drinks, holding the baby, and so on.
- Accept help from family members with a thankful spirit.
- To make cleanup quicker, use paper plates and napkins.
- Choose easy-to-prepare foods, such as cook-ahead casseroles, raw vegetables and dip (creamy Italian salad dressing makes a great dip), or Stouffer's Frozen Lasagna (both meat and vegetarian are delicious, and everyone will think you made it from scratch).

Getting Together When You Live in the Same Town

If you live in the same town as some or all of your extended family, you will have lots of opportunities to get together with your loved ones. We strongly suggest a regular extended-family gathering, whether once a week or once a month. Don't wait on your parents or others to organize this gathering. Take responsibility for planning a potluck dinner, picnic, or breakfast, lunch, or dinner out together.

Sometimes we have chosen to stay in a nearby hotel when visiting our children. This gives us a place to retreat to and take a nap—or often we bring the grandchildren with us for a swim in the hotel pool. Once, when we got a really good rate, we reserved two rooms and invited our son and his family to spend the night at the hotel with us. We all went swimming together, and it was great fun for all of us and especially for our grandchildren. While we couldn't afford to do this regularly, it was a fun treat and great memory maker!

—DAVE AND CLAUDIA

FAMILY REUNIONS

Family reunions are making a comeback as kinfolk gather to celebrate the past, enjoy the present, and look forward to the future. Jennifer Crichton wrote: "Reunions can be a time and place where relationships out of kilter can be put back on track again. Where what has been dangling can be connected. Where those most prone to being outside looking in can be drawn across the threshold and into the heart of the family."[1] Isn't that something we all desire?

According to our survey participants, families get together for reunions in myriad ways. Some get together for one day each year. Others meet every two or three years, and some get together for several days. Some family reunions are always held at the old family home place. Other meet at a campground or another neutral location. All seem to want to reconnect with one another and make the time and distance that separates them recede. They want to forget their cares and be family once again.

What we gleaned from our survey is there is no one way to pull off a family reunion. So if your heart is leading you to organize your own family reunion, let us encourage you to pursue it.[2] We've gathered a few suggestions from others, which we pass on to you.

- Make a genealogical chart to sort out who's who on the different limbs and branches of your family tree. It will be a conversation starter with relatives you don't know so well.
- Use nametags and code them with the names of your parents and grandparents.

The first time we entertained Dave's parents, we had only been married one week. His parents were heading back to Naples, Italy, where they were stationed in the military, and stopped by our tiny basement apartment. Boy, was I nervous! I don't remember what I served them, but I do remember Dave's mom's accepting smile. She was just happy to be there. Food and how I served it were the least of her concerns. Over the years as we have visited our adult children, I've tried to have the same accepting smile and attitude that Dave's mom so often gave to me.

—DAVE AND CLAUDIA

- Take a group photograph.
- You might want to order T-shirts for everyone with the family name and date of the reunion.
- Consider buying the main part of the meal and then asking everyone else to bring side dishes or desserts.
- One survey participant wrote, "Singing together as a family is my favorite part of the reunion."
- Set up a family Web page and invite everyone to post messages. It will be a great way to stay in touch after the reunion and get the word out about the next one.

LIFE CELEBRATIONS

Many get-togethers occur around "life celebrations." Weddings and funerals are the most common and most memorable of these life celebrations, but you could also think here about births, baptisms, confirmations, or graduations. Not all life celebrations are the same; for example, funerals are often sad and are usually planned in just a few days, whereas weddings are usually planned months in advance and are happy events. However, life celebrations share a common opportunity to bring extended families together to celebrate a life or lives—even if it's the end of one.

Weddings

Weddings are certainly one of the most-often-cited answers to the survey question "What are your favorite extended-family activities?" When a family prepares for a wedding and extended-family members are included, it can become a de facto family reunion. Grandparents, aunts, uncles, cousins, nieces, nephews, and grandchildren all converge to celebrate a life mile-marker for the bride and groom. Unlike family reunions, however, the occasion being celebrated belongs to the bride and groom, and all extended-family members should remember that they are guests at this event and certain, set rules of etiquette apply. Weddings are not the time to engage in old family squabbles or settle religious or political differences. As we have said before, if ever there is a time to settle for polite chitchat—weddings would surely be the time.

By the time the wedding week rolls around, there often has been much emotional turmoil endured by the bride, groom, and respective families. On top of this, one must remember that a great deal of resources—time, money, thought, planning—have been dedicated to this event and the stakes are high. Therefore, peace at almost any cost is the highest priority.

One interesting thing we have noticed over the years is that no matter how much money, time, and effort have gone into planning a wedding, something always seems to go wrong—a relative dies the day before the wedding or a hurricane blows in or the preacher gets the name wrong or the air conditioning at the church goes out. Don't let a little blunder or sudden storm ruin the big day. Expect something to go wrong, plan for it, deal with it, get through it, and laugh about it later!

Funerals and Family Crises

We were surprised that a top response to the "What draws the extended family together?" question in our survey was funerals and family crises. Hard times do tend to pull families together. When we face the reality of the death or serious illness of a loved one, little grievances seem less significant. At such times people take the time to reflect on life and think about what is really important. Because family members tend to be more open in times of crisis, you may be able to use these times to repair relationships and build bridges.

Funerals. It is important to remember that funerals—unlike weddings—are generally not planned out very well and, in most cases, it is not clear who is in charge. Power struggles occasionally emerge over things like casket color and what hymns to sing. Who assumes the leadership role? Then there is the

---

One of the major conflicts that surfaces at weddings is: Whose "party" is it? The marriage is between the bride and the groom, but most often the parents of the bride or some other party pay for "the big day" and rightfully expect to have some say in the important decisions. It is best if the family can work together peacefully; however, if (or should we say "when"?) serious conflict erupts, a good general rule is to let the bride and groom have final say over the wedding ceremony, and whoever is paying for the reception should have ultimate control of it.

issue of money and financing: How much does all this cost, and who should pay? Did the deceased have insurance to cover the expenses? What is in the will? Who gets what? Death and funerals are stressful events. Therefore, be sensitive to the feelings of everybody, and be forgiving and understanding. You don't do this very often!

Generally, there is less chitchat at funerals: Funeral gatherings provide for a healthy swap of family history (warm memories) and life updates from relatives who have not been seen in months or years. You might want to consider updating the old concept of a wake and have a party in memory of the deceased. After one funeral I (John) performed, the sons of the deceased gave a party for 500 people! They asked to have a microphone turned on and they told stories and invited others to come forward and do the same. The storytelling lasted almost three hours, but time went by rapidly. Everybody laughed much and cried hard.

Tips for holding a wake include:

• Have the wake at a home, club, or restaurant (not at the funeral home or church).
• Do it immediately after the funeral, if at all possible.
• Invite everybody (not just family).
• Have it catered (by professionals or friends).
• If some friends offer to help, say yes.
• Take the phone off the hook when it's over.
• Split the costs among all family members.

Death and life together. Occasionally, happy events—such as weddings— occur at the same time as a painful event—such as the death of a loved one or the conspicuous absence of an alienated relative. I (John) have performed a funeral for a family one day and a wedding in that same family the very next day. If you're ever faced with a similar situation, I recommend that you find an appropriate time to acknowledge the loss or grief. In so doing, you have named the grief but you have not let it overwhelm you. As Christians, we are to grieve, but "not like the rest of men, who have no hope" (1 Thessalonians 4:13).

Recently, I conducted a wedding for a young groom who had lost both of his parents a few months prior to the wedding weekend. Working with his fiancée, we agreed that the appropriate thing to do was to go to the grave marker after the wedding rehearsal on Friday night with other close relatives and have a brief memorial service. This enabled him to acknowledge their absence and his grief without totally eclipsing the joy of his wedding day.

Other times of distress. Other times of crisis or distress afford the opportunity to draw closer to your extended family. On the first anniversary of the September 11th terrorist attacks, we (Dave and Claudia) chose to spend the day with our family who lives closest to us. We spent a few hours together and shared a meal and then drove home. The six hours we spent in the car going and coming that day were well worth the opportunity to be with our family, and during the drive we talked at length about our own extended family and how much they mean to us.

MAJOR HOLIDAYS = MAJOR EXPECTATIONS

Getting the whole family clan together to celebrate a holiday can present challenges as well as opportunities. Ask anyone you know what their first thought is when you say Thanksgiving, Christmas, Easter, or the Fourth of July. You most likely will receive as many different answers as your number of respondents. They can be the best of times or the worst of times. Major tension can erupt over the question "Where should we go for the holidays?"

When we (Dave and Claudia) were first married, we celebrated Christmas in Ellijay, Georgia, where Claudia's parents lived. Dave's grandmother and aunts also lived in Ellijay. Fortunately, they were all friends, so we would all get together for our holiday feast—but we also made the rounds to each relative's home for an expected visit. Dave's parents lived in Naples, Italy, so it was easy to initially answer the "where" question for Thanksgiving and Christmas holidays. Ellijay was it!

Later, when we had children, the first few years we continued to make the Christmas pilgrimage to Ellijay. Then we made a decision that wasn't exactly popular with our families. We decided to celebrate Christmas in our own home and invited parents and grandparents to come and join. For us that worked quite well until we moved to Europe. When we lived in Europe, we included other families and single adults in our holiday celebration. Once when John Bell was in college, he and his traveling buddy, Stubbs, were two of the singles at our Christmas dinner table!

When we (John and Margaret) were first married, before we had children and before John was officially serving a church, we took the simple alternating approach. We would spend Thanksgiving with one set of parents and Christmas with the other and simply alternate from year to year. And then ... our first child entered the picture and John was called to serve a congregation.

We figured out that if we wanted to have any extended-family time around the holidays, we should invite everyone to our house. Thus, for several years we would have various assortments of relatives coming and going in the days and weeks surrounding Christmas. I (Margaret) look back upon that time with fond recollection and many happy memories. The only way that system worked was our unwritten policy that any help was welcome help. So family members would show up armed with food or an offer to help shop and cook, or to watch the children and keep them entertained, or in several instances to contribute financially. It also helped enormously that we were relatively young with quite a bit of energy and stamina!

What to Do When Family Can't Come?

One year when we (John and Margaret) were in Mississippi, our church had a significant community-wide ecumenical service that John did not want to miss as the pastor, so we invited both sides of the family to come for Thanksgiving. However, neither family could join us. We ended up inviting some dear friends from out of town whom we had not seen in a while and joined forces with some friends down the street who could not travel to see their families because of a new baby. In the end, we created one of our favorite Thanksgiving memories of all.

We decided to go all out with the china and the silver and the linen and a full-blown, bona fide southern Thanksgiving menu. Accordingly, everyone dressed up for the midafternoon feast and pitched in with the cleanup afterward. Once the dishes were washed and put away and the plentiful leftovers dealt with, we took a group walk and found other folks looking for fresh air and arranged a fabulous co-ed, touch football game where all were welcome. It was a day-long party and celebration that none of us will soon forget.

Many other families celebrate major holidays by dividing the day between their families of origin. Turkey and pumpkin pie for both lunch and dinner give new meaning to the saying "feast or famine"! Jill and Larry and their two kids spend the first half of Christmas with Jill's mom and the second half with Larry's parents. But Larry's parents are disappointed that no one ever seems to take second servings and the children seem to pick at their food.

When the day is over, no one is really satisfied—least of all Jill and Larry's children, who would love to be home with their new toys. What could they do that might be more obliging for all? One suggestion would be to combine families and include Jill's mom one year with Larry's parents' celebration and switch off the next year. Perhaps Jill and Larry could also take their turn at hosting Christmas dinner.

Mandy and Jeff's parents live 200 miles away in opposite directions. Their solution is to go to one parents' home one year and to the other parents' home the next. One year their whole extended family met at a conference center for the holidays. They got a great deal on rooms because it was a down time for the conference center, and everyone was on neutral ground.

If you look long and hard enough, you will probably be able to find a compromise with which everyone can live.

THANKSGIVING

On the Wednesday before Thanksgiving, people all across America still embark on an annual pilgrimage toward some sort of traditional family gathering to celebrate this major national holiday with extended family. Travel experts claim that the day before Thanksgiving is the busiest travel day of the year. Airports offer long lines; bus and train stations are jammed; the highways are clogged. And, generally, if folks are not traveling, they are probably cleaning and cooking or performing minor home repairs.

If you know tension exists in your family clan, consider inviting friends outside the family to join you for the celebration. Also remember that while holiday get-togethers are wonderful, if you are too dogmatic or inflexible, these times together can simply increase conflict and tension. So don't mix demands and subtle attempts to manipulate with a family event that is supposed to be a fun celebration. Flexibility is the best policy!

However, we suspect that for most people in America, travel plans, dining arrangements, and accommodations do not give rise to as much anxiety as do the various emotional and spiritual challenges of gathering as an extended family. Thanksgiving is a time to express our gratitude for the blessings that we have been given, but it is not always completely obvious that our extended family is a wonderful blessing for which we should be thankful. Extended-family gatherings can be wonderful, but they are frequently fraught with tension.

Gloria Scott grew up having Thanksgiving dinner at her grandparents' house every year, and for her that memory is worth the effort to preserve that tradition. In a sense it is her gift to her children and grandchildren even though they may not yet see it in that light. The culture has changed radically since Gloria was a child, but the core value of the extended family sharing the Thanksgiving meal is the catalyst.

Think about what the first Thanksgiving meal must have looked like, or your great-great-great-grandparents' Thanksgiving, or your grandparents'. The recurrent image is the gathering of family and friends around a table to share a meal. Decorations, guests' attire, formality or informality of dining, and menu choices are not the most important part of an extended family holiday. The most important part is being together.

Thanksgiving in Austria

Did you ever consider that Thanksgiving is uniquely an American holiday? We (Dave and Claudia) didn't until we lived in Vienna, Austria, and our three sons attended a British school. Imagine having to go to school on Thanksgiving! And we soon discovered our British friends had a completely different perspective about Thanksgiving. We talked of the Pilgrims who came to America seeking religious freedom and a chance to have a new start. Our British friends talked about rebellion!

Actually, Thanksgiving should be a universal Christian holiday. Throughout the Scriptures, we are admonished to remember what God has done for us and to be thankful. In 1 Samuel 12:24 we read, "But be sure to fear the LORD and serve him faithfully with all your heart; consider what great things he has done for you." How can we help our extended family express gratitude to God for all the great things He has done for us? One way is to include others who are less fortunate in our family Thanksgiving celebration. During the five years our family lived in Austria, we began a new tradition. While we missed our own extended family, we compensated by inviting friends to our Thanksgiving celebration. Each year our friends Jody and Linda Dillow and their four children joined us for our thankful feast. Our children were around the same ages, and the Dillow children reminded us of cousins far away in the United States. We would also invite others who were lonely or away from their families to join us. One year we included a well-known pastor from Poland, who was amazed at the bounty on our table, and we were enthralled with hearing the courageous experiences of Christians in Poland. In our Thanksgiving memory bank, that is one of our best-ever Thanksgivings.

When we moved back to the States we resumed the more traditional Thanksgiving celebration, and Claudia's parents and Dave's aunt would join us in Knoxville, Tennessee. I (Claudia) remember being so exhausted as I tried to do it all. I attempted to prepare all our family's favorite dishes from Austria as well as those of our extended family. One day I realized that no one ate the creamed celery that had always been on my grandmother's Thanksgiving table. That was the end of that tradition.

Everyone has his or her own ideas about which traditions associated with holidays are of vital importance. I (Margaret) vividly remember my twenty-second Thanksgiving. For my first 21 Thanksgivings, along with the turkey, dressing, gravy, mashed potatoes, green beans, corn pudding, and rolls with strawberry butter, we had sweet potatoes with marshmallows melted on top and pumpkin pie with whipped cream. Well, since this was my first Thanksgiving with my new husband and his family, you can imagine my utter shock and disbelief when not only did we not have sweet potatoes with dinner—we didn't even have pumpkin pie with whipped cream for dessert. I remember crying over this at the time and am grateful that after 19 additional Thanksgivings, I can look back on that one and laugh.

Sharing the Load

The Lewis family was planning to meet at the grandparents' home for Thanksgiving and would include the grandparents, three grown daughters, sons-in-law, and eight grandchildren. Recognizing that everyone might have different ideas about what constitutes the Thanksgiving meal, the grandmother asked via e-mail well in advance what each couple would like to contribute to the meal. In this way, everyone's favorite thing could be included.

For one it was squash casserole; for another, a pecan pie; and for a third it was a fresh organic turkey.

Fun Extended-Family Thanksgiving Activities

When several generations are together, it's a great time for a few planned activities. We suggest the following:

- *Make an "I'm thankful" list.* Take turns adding to your "I'm thankful" list. Start with the youngest family member and work up to the oldest. See how many things you can think of. Photocopy the list and give a copy to each family represented at your gathering to take home.
- *Write a Thanksgiving prayer.* Choose an "intergenerational committee" to compose a special prayer to share at dinner.
- *String Cranberries.* With a blunt needle and coarse thread, let the children string cranberries. Put the strings on trees in the yard for the birds.
- *Practice peacemaking.* Take a few moments to think about people in your life (this may include extended-family members) who may not be easy to get along with. Talk about how the Pilgrims and Indians made peace. Think about how different they were from each other and how that would complicate things. Think of at least one nice thing you can do for someone with whom you find it hard to get along.
- *Make life-size Indians and Pilgrims.* Tape together two pieces of newsprint and trace around the young children in the family. Let the children color and decorate the silhouette as a Pilgrim or an Indian. Cut out and put them on the wall. Talk about whom you identify with the most—the Indians or the Pilgrims. Why?

Four Tips for Hosting Your Holiday Dinner

1. Plan your seating arrangement carefully. Don't put two relatives together who you know will start bickering.
2. Make the day children-friendly. Have pre-dinner activities and include food that children will enjoy.
3. After dinner organize a family walk.
4. Don't expect perfection.

- *Make Mayflower baskets.* Decorate a basket and fill it with goodies that an elderly friend could use, such as fruit, nuts, stationery, stamps, and assorted cards. Take the basket to an elderly friend or neighbor. Put the basket by the door. Ring the doorbell and hide!
- *Decorate the first Christmas tree.* A fun Arp grandmother-grandchild Thanksgiving tradition is making Christmas tree decorations with each grandchild. Together we decorate Oma's little Christmas tree. Then as the grandkids leave, each takes a couple of the decorations he or she made to put on his or her own tree at home, leaving several for Oma and Opa's pre-Christmas tree.

CHRISTMAS

Following right on the heels of Thanksgiving is Christmas, the other major extended-family holiday. Actually, Christmas holidays are being pushed by stores as early as September or October. Do you ever feel someone rewrote the Christmas script like this: "And it came to pass in those days that there went out a decree from the trendsetters, the advertising agencies, and the Joneses down the street that all of America should go shopping. And all went out to shop, each to his own mall." Instead of peace on earth and goodwill toward humanity, many people find themselves in a frenzied cycle of working, spending, and preparing that accelerates right up until the first SUV pulls into the driveway.

It's easy to feel stress at this time of year—especially if the entire family is coming to your house for the holidays. You still remember last year when the cousins fought over their presents, the dog ate the pumpkin pie, and Aunt Gertrude wouldn't speak to Uncle Albert. One reason for holiday stress is wanting everything to be wonderful and for all the extended family to unite in perfect harmony. We picture one big happy family gathered around the tree surrounded by just the right gifts. Snowflakes gracefully fall outside, while inside the aromas of turkey, ham, and mincemeat pie fill the house—which, of course, is immaculate and looks like the December issue of *House Beautiful.*

If you are hoping for a storybook Christmas this year, let us remind you that storybook holidays should be reserved for the pages of storybooks! How can we keep our expectations realistic? If the whole family clan is planning to celebrate at your house, there is hope—you can practice the three P's of a peaceful Christmas—pray, plan, and persevere.

Pray

Never underestimate the power of prayer—especially when it comes to extended-family holiday celebrations. When we are prayerfully considering our family times together, we will be more sensitive to others and will look for God's guidance in relating to family members. In James 1:5 we read that if we lack wisdom we are to ask God for it, and He will give it to us liberally. So start by praying for each family member who will be coming for the holidays, including yourself!

Plan

Plan the logistics. Part of planning is deciding where, with whom, and when you will be getting together for Christmas. If your extended family is like ours, we're not the only family on the block hosting Christmas, so we have to be willing to share. One significant tension from our survey is the issue of "Where do we go for Christmas?" and "What if we simply want to stay home?" The key word we would suggest in planning for Christmas get-togethers is *flexibility*.

"We celebrate holidays whenever we can get together and don't go by the calendar. Once we had Christmas in July!"

—SURVEY RESPONDENT

"We split the holidays. Every year our side of the family gets together for Thanksgiving; Christmas is for the other side of the family. This plan has worked fine for over 20 years!"

—SURVEY RESPONDENT

From one grandmother: "I have a permanent Christmas room with a Christmas tree with lights, and small gifts under the tree. My grandchildren know it is always Christmas at our home."

Over the years we have been creative in celebrating Christmas as an extended family. For several years, the Arps met at Crested Butte, Colorado, a couple of weeks before Christmas when it was inexpensive to rent condos and the skiing was free. One family we know has Christmas in July at the beach. You might want to put your heads together with your family and see what creative ideas you come up with.

Plan to be flexible. When we visit others in our family for Christmas, we try to fit into their traditions—some of which are different from the ones our sons grew up observing. When the Arp family clan comes to us for Christmas we've learned to be flexible, but not too flexible. One Christmas stands out in our memory. Traditionally we always attend the midnight candle-lighting service at our church. On this particular Christmas Eve, some in our family wanted to attend another church, so we said, "Fine, we'll go with you." Then no one could agree. In the end, we didn't make it to any of the services. Now, we just announce what we are doing and let the others decide for themselves what service they want to (or don't want to) participate in.

Plan purposeful traditions. Neither of us (Dave and Claudia) came from families with lots of traditions. As we previously mentioned, we lived in Austria when our children were growing up, so we built our own family traditions—some from our extended family, but many from the Austrian culture. Some were precious especially to me (Claudia). When our sons began to marry and have children of their own, our traditions began to change. I experienced anew what Solomon wrote in Ecclesiastes, "There is a time for everything.... A time to tear down and a time to build" (3:1, 3). We might paraphrase and say that there is a time for building traditions and a time for letting go. Also, observing a tradition doesn't mean you have to do the same thing the same way every year. One year we had a Christmas tree ornament factory and as family and friends arrived, they would decorate their very own wax Christmas tree decoration. (More on traditions later.)

Plan family activities. If the gang is coming to your house for Christmas, take our advice and be prepared with some fun family activities. Following are some of our favorites:

- *Make a yearly family scrapbook.* Pull out all the favorite snapshots from the past year and arrange them in a scrapbook. In the coming years, it will be fun to look through all the scrapbooks from years gone by. Actually, we (Dave and Claudia) like to bring out scrapbooks from years ago. Grandkids love looking at pictures of their dad when he was their age.

- *Make dough ornaments.* Mix together 2 cups flour, 1 cup salt, and 1 cup water. Knead together. Roll out and cut with cookies cutters; brush with beaten egg. Punch a hole in each ornament before baking. Bake at 300 degrees.

Push red and green yarn or ribbon through the hole and make a tie for each ornament. Leave the ornaments natural or paint them with acrylic paints. Spray varnish for a lovely finish.

- *Take a holiday tour of lights.* Take a tour of your community. Let the kids plan the route. If you are really energetic, make it a walking tour.
- *Have a brown bag party.* Have an impromptu brown bag family Christmas party. Roll down the tops of brown lunch bags, and fill each bag with goodies to munch around the tree. You could use nuts, dried fruit, popcorn, miniature muffins, and cookies. Put on your favorite Christmas CD, light the tree, and take a few minutes to enjoy each other and the wonder of this time of year.
- *Set up a game table.* Pull out your favorite games and have them available for those who would like to play. Call family members ahead of time and ask, "What are the current best sellers?" and have a couple of new games ready to be opened.
- *Celebrate Christmas afternoon.* Take time to wind down. Pull out a Christmas puzzle to do after all the presents are open and the meal is over. Also, you could pull out sleeping bags and foam pads and take a family nap around the Christmas tree.

Persevere

Realize that major holidays will come with their share of stresses. Kids get hyper. Siblings revert to their adolescent ways. In-laws sometimes don't feel included. Parents and grandparents may be tired and cranky. The closest I (Claudia) ever came to resigning from the human race and definitely from being a family-life educator was one Christmas when I was having a hard time persevering. It was our first Christmas with married children, and I won't bore you with the details, but everyone seemed to be missing each other's expectations—especially mine. After the holidays, I was comparing stories with a friend who is a number of years ahead of us in family life, and she confided, "This was actually our first Christmas without tears." So wherever you are in your extended family ladder, there is hope. Persevere!

And remember, Christmas isn't just about you and your extended family. It's a great opportunity to reach out to others in your community, like the wonderful family matriarch in the following story.

Reaching Out Beyond Family

We (John and Margaret) will never forget our first Christmas in Columbus, Georgia. One family in our church had an indomitable matriarch leader, who for years and years had two holiday traditions that are still observed by the next generations and will be far into the future. Every year our church had a beautiful Christmas Lessons and Carols service on the Sunday night before Christmas, and this dear lady decided that was the perfect time for her to host her extended family Christmas dinner. Her grown and married children and their grown and growing children, and their children as well as all the aunts, uncles, sisters, brothers, and cousins, along with the minister and his family, were invited to her home for dinner.

Every year—no matter what the temperature outside—she had fires in the fireplaces, candles lit, Christmas decorations, fresh greenery and flowers, and a beautiful silver ornament for every guest. Everyone knew how important and special this occasion was and would not miss it if humanly possible, because she made everyone feel welcome and loved.

When things get stressful during the holidays:

- Take a warm bath. Warm water calms you by increasing circulation and relaxing muscles.
- Breathe deeply. When anxiety strikes, the heart races; breathing deeply will help you relax.
- Build a fire, turn on soft music, and have a cup of hot chocolate or tea.
- Have a quiet time. Read your favorite passage of Scripture or Psalm 23.
- Keep your sense of humor.
- Write in a journal. Sometimes summing up the day's highs and lows will help you laugh at them and keep things in perspective.

The other tradition associated with this special annual occasion was the unwritten code of behavior that everyone from the youngest child to the great uncle seemed to intuitively understand. Everybody dressed in their finest holiday attire and had attitudes that matched. All chose to be on their best behavior and get along with everyone. Each one helped keep the party lively and light and truly joyous by recounting aloud memories from past holidays or telling funny stories that had occurred during the year, or by simply sharing the newest joke.

You see, one person can make a huge difference by her actions—it was her joy and enthusiasm and happiness at having those nearest and dearest to her together and her generous hospitality that were her gift to all of us.

Now let's turn our attention to those traditions and rituals that become part of the fabric of extended family. How do they develop and how do they change over the years?

Building Extended Family Traditions and Rituals

For many extended families, the traditions that revolve around certain holidays and celebrations are what family members cherish about their experience. However, as the extended family changes and evolves, family members may not be willing to maintain, fully support, or take leadership in preserving these traditions.

From our observations, the women in the family have typically been the keepers of traditions and the maintainers of extended-family relationships—especially in the older generation. In our generation (Dave and Claudia's), women tend to be the ones who remember birthdays, anniversaries, shop for Christmas presents, and plan the reunions and vacations. But this is changing with the younger generation and calls for a reordering of priorities by each nuclear family and clear communication among all.

Andrea, 25, and Carl, 28, have been married for two years. Each takes care of keeping up with birthdays and buying gifts for their own family. Unfortunately, Carl is absentminded and often forgets his family while Andrea is diligent about remembering her own family's special days. This is already creating tension with Carl's family. They don't understand why Andrea doesn't take the initiative in remembering their special days.

Sometimes individual families don't realize how important a particular tradition is to the rest of the family—especially to those in a different generation. Also, we need to remember that traditions are not static and that we may need to make adjustments as circumstances change and as the years go by.

HOLIDAY TRADITIONS

"I'll never forget a conversation with Marcy the first Christmas season after she married my son, Rob," commented one mother-in-law. "Marcy called to ask how to make felt Christmas tree ornaments. There's a history to this request. In discussing how to decorate their apartment for the holidays, Marcy asked Rob, 'What theme to you want for the Christmas tree—Victorian, English, or country?'

"'Theme?' replied Rob. 'You don't have a theme—you make everything!' So Marcy was calling me to ask how to make the felt ornaments Rob talked about."

When new families are formed, we all need to remember that two family traditions must blend together. This can create tension between the generations. Parents need to encourage the younger families to choose traditions that they are comfortable with and to accept the fact that they will probably drop some favorite traditions. The younger generation needs to be sensitive to those traditions their parents consider dear—especially when they spend the holidays with their parents.

After the conversation with Marcy, Rob's mother went through her tree decorations. Sure enough, they had made many of them as a family. She chose some that her son had made and others that were his favorites and sent them to Marcy and Rob. It was her little way of sharing some of the family's traditions with the next generation.

Perhaps you identify with this mother-in-law. She wanted to pass on traditions, but she wanted to be sensitive and not overstep. It's only natural that parents would desire to pass on traditions, but when it is force-fed to the next generation, it becomes manipulative, and that's one tradition none of us wants to pass on.

There are nonmanipulative ways to encourage the younger generation to continue family traditions. One Arp favorite Christmas tradition is lighting the candles on our Austrian nativity pyramid. One year we found the same kind of pyramid on sale, so we bought three—one for each of our sons to have when they established their own home. This tradition was received with appreciation and gratitude.

BIRTHDAY TRADITIONS

Some families place a high value on celebrating birthdays or anniversaries or graduations, and others do not. Understanding the experiences or expectations of your extended-family members can be an important part of your relationship.

Perhaps your daughter-in-law grew up being queen for a day on her birthday or your son-in-law doesn't even remember what day his birthday is until someone wishes him a good one. Maybe you have—or are—parents or grandparents who have not missed one graduation or confirmation or baptism. On the other hand, many family members think a phone call or a card conveys all that is needed on certain occasions. Communicating with your extended-family members about these experiences or expectations can avert a lot of hurt feelings or misunderstandings before they ever happen. Survey respondents show that celebrating birthdays as an extended family is a favorite tradition to many.

The Crawford family has two June birthdays within a week of each other. They have taken their family vacation every year for 10 years in June at the grandparents' beach home, and one night has always been designated the birthday celebration night complete with one chocolate and one vanilla birthday cake. This time alone with the grandparents became a Crawford tra-

Ways to Encourage the Blending of Traditions

- Pass on special mementos from childhood.
- Create a journal of traditions from your parents and grandparents. Include the ones you dropped—the younger generation may be interested in them.
- Repeat each day: "A rejection of my traditions is not a rejection of me."

dition. It was special because the birthday kids had all of the grandparents' attention—it was just them, their parents, and the grandparents.

Then one year this tradition was interrupted. Here's what happened. The birthday night had been carefully planned to accommodate everyone's fairly complicated schedules and could not be altered. Then others in the family, who in the past were not part of this tradition and had always left before the birthdays, decided to extend their time and stay a couple of more days at the beach. Since their children's birthdays were also coming up soon, the plans were changed to include everyone. Well, the grandparents were caught in the middle and a win-win situation could not be reached. The birthday tradition was broken and hurt feelings ensued.

A tip: As close as extended families sometimes are, the nuclear family will be closer. Never compete with the nuclear family. You won't win. The mother and daddy bears will do all they can do to protect their cubs. While the intention was to honor all the birthdays that were coming up, the Crawford parents were first concerned about their own two children and their disappointment that the 10-year-long tradition was being broken. Sometimes, as was the case here, it is no one's fault. Things happen—even with the best-laid plans. So at times like this, remember the rule "Be flexible, love, and forgive." Family is more important than birthdays. The Crawford family is a strong family, and they weathered this small crisis. So like the Crawfords, when traditions get broken, do all you can not to break family relationships.

Birthdays at the Arps'

Birthdays are more important to some than to others. At the Arps', birthdays are really important to Claudia and not as important to Dave. So guess whose birthday gets ignored the most? Dave's? Wrong! Claudia's? Right. Some in our family are better about remembering than others. And at times they really do them up great.

Make a list of traditions you observe, and note the origin of each. Then ask yourself, "Which of these are no longer meaningful?" Finally, make a list of traditions you would like to start.

Recently we were all at the beach together. My (Claudia's) birthday—we won't say which one but it was a big one—was coming up the next week, and it would be a good time to celebrate it as a family. I just tried not to get my hopes up too high. I was a bit suspicious when they sent Dave and me off to the latest Disney movie with all the grandkids. Still, I was really surprised to walk into the beach house fully decorated for my birthday. But the real highlight was the gift that my sons, daughters-in-law, and grandkids gave to me—a PowerPoint presentation (played on my son's laptop computer) with a video of everyone—including the babies—giving me tips for the next decade of life and generally acting silly. Also included in the presentation was a wonderful collection of digital pictures set to music from our time together at the beach. Far more precious than gifts they could go out and buy, this special "I love you" covers them at least until next Christmas! Speaking of gifts, read on.

The Meaning of Gifts

Birthday as well as Christmas gift giving may be a significant issue for your extended family to deal with. Paul Tournier, the noted Swiss psychologist, wrote that one can dominate others through gifts. Certainly we don't want to use gifts to try to manipulate or control others. We also need to note that for some, Christmas gift giving can be an overwhelming experience financially, physically, and emotionally for the giver as well as the receiver.

Many families choose to set limits on Christmas gifts by drawing names, limiting dollar amounts, exchanging only homemade gifts, and/or choosing to bestow significant and meaningful gifts for birthdays when there may not be so much chaos. Once again, as we saw with the Scotts, not every family will automatically agree on the best way to go about gift giving.

While we are on the topic of gift giving it is important to remember that it truly is "the thought that counts." A new daughter-in-law in one family had married into a relatively large extended family and recognized the importance of knowing when birthdays and anniversaries of her new extended family members occur. Spurred on by her Christmas budget constraints, she put her computer skills to work and made a calendar with family pictures, carefully marking everyone's birthdays and anniversaries, and gave one to each family. Her thoughtful gift was appreciated by all and has become something everyone looks forward to receiving each Christmas.

It is important to remember that as we get older, birthdays do not become less important. No one is ever too old or too young to be remembered or fussed over on his or her birthday. If you are a younger generation adult, don't fall into the trap of thinking that your parents or grandparents enjoy celebrating their children's or grandchildren's birthdays but don't look forward to reciprocation when their own special day rolls around. That is not an intergenerational relationship builder!

Thank You, Thank You, Thank You!

Thank-you notes remain a hot topic for parents to this day. I (Margaret) still remember not being allowed to play with any new toys or gifts the day after Christmas or my birthday until I had written the appropriate thank-you notes. Now that I am a parent, I have a better understanding of the intricacies associated with this issue. I have not successfully instilled the same rule for thank-you notes for my daughters, but we do all recognize the importance of timely gratitude. A favorite quote related to this issue is "Gratitude delayed is gratitude denied."

Another great reason for writing thank-you notes is that if your extended family doesn't regularly communicate, thank-you notes are a way of simply acknowledging that a gift arrived.

No Strings Attached

On the other side of the spectrum is the gift given with certain strings attached. This is not healthy and should be avoided at all costs. Such a gift often ends up costing both giver and receiver a price beyond monetary value—feelings are hurt as expectations are not met and the relationship suffers. Relationships cannot be bought with money and things. Relationships develop with time, thoughtfulness, and care. Give gifts because you want to—not to get a thank-you note or to have the recipient feel beholden to you. Gifts are a symbol of your affection and care for those you love and do not require huge sums of money to be deemed thoughtful or found meaningful.

If your birthday goes unnoticed by your family for whatever reason, we suggest you do have an option. Buy yourself a gift—recognize outwardly and symbolically that you are a child of God, valued and loved—and make your day special for yourself. So be the adult; give a little slack and forgiveness if others forget your birthday.

Whether you are getting together to celebrate a birthday, holiday, family vacation, or just sharing a meal together, we encourage you to look for ways to promote harmony. Times together will aid you in building positive relationships with the whole family clan.

Give age-appropriate gifts. We know your grandkid is brilliant and advanced, but just humor us on this one. You'll thank us, and so will the parents of your grandkids. When toys are too advanced, the child becomes bored and will never use it, even later when it would be age-appropriate.

—DAVE AND CLAUDIA

Challenge Five

Challenge Five

Fostering Positive Relationships in the Clan

When we asked our kids and Dave and Claudia's grandkids what were the best times with their cousins, grandparents, and aunts and uncles, we heard things like:

- Playing in the stream with my cousins at our grandparents' house and building a tent out of sheets.
- Getting lost with Oma and Opa (the Arps) walking around Lake Harriet trying to find Ron's Market.
- Sledding down the mountain at Elk River in North Carolina with my parents (the Bells) and visiting friends.
- Going crabbing after dark with my cousins, aunts, uncles, and Opa on the beaches at the Outer Banks of North Carolina.
- Making wax Christmas tree decorations with Oma at Thanksgiving and decorating the little Christmas tree with my cousins.
- Hiking together in the North Georgia Mountains with my family and grandparents and charting our own path without getting lost.

Amazingly, as we listened to our children and grandchildren, most of the cherished memories were simple times together with cousins, siblings, and other extended-family members. Few required an investment of money and resources. All required an investment of time—of just being intentional and grabbing the moments together.

What would be your best memories of times together with your extended family? How would your children and/or grandchildren answer our question? We would guess that, like our families, the best memories would not be the expensive trips or gifts you may have given them. While in the last challenge we saw that gift giving can be a positive part of great extended-family relationships, money and gifts are no substitute for time.

Bottom line, you can't buy great memories or healthy relationships with your children, grandchildren, grandparents, or others in your family clan. But the good news is that you can build positive relationships and wonderful memories. In the last challenge, we looked at family get-togethers and how to make them positive and peaceful. In this challenge, we explore several ways to begin to deepen the relationships and build fun memories when we get together with other extended-family members: grandkids and grandparents; adult children and parents; adult siblings and spouses; and cousins, aunts, and uncles. Let's start with that most precious relationship between grandparents and grandchildren.

GRANDPARENTS AND GRANDCHILDREN

Someone has said that the reason grandparents and grandkids get along so well is that they have a common enemy. While we would hope this is not true, we do observe a special bond between grandparents and grandchildren. Over the years, grandparents have played an important role in the lives of their grandchildren. But today's grandparents are very different from those in past generations.

You Don't Look Like a Grandmother is the name of a hilarious play based on some valid observations of our present world. Today's extended family doesn't look like the extended family of 50 years ago. Grandparents tend to be younger and more active. According to the National Center for Health Statistics, the average age for becoming a grandmother in the year 2000 was 47. That's young! Nor do today's grandmothers have "permed blue hair and half-bushel hips wrapped in aprons." Today's grandmothers are just as likely "to have spiky blond hair and hard-muscled glutes wrapped in tight exercise pants," observes author and social trends observer Gail Sheehy.

Grandparenthood is a defining moment—a grand passage. However, it's one you can't plan, choose, or postpone and often comes as a surprise. But Sheehy sees becoming a grandparent as a wonderful passage. "Grandchildren soften our hearts. They loosen the sludge of old resentments and regrets. It's a chance for reconciliation between ourselves and our children."[1]

The way to your children's hearts just may be through your grandchildren. And the converse is true. When you have children, it's a chance for reconciliation with your parents and older generations. Having children gives new insights into what it may have been like for your own parents when you were born. So for both generations, children offer great opportunities to connect with and enjoy family. We just have to look for them.

Treasured Memories

I (Margaret) remember when I used to go visit my grandmother by myself every summer. It was such an adventure to fly alone, and when I arrived at my grandmother's house she had a scavenger hunt game for me that ended in the room where I was to stay. It was such a creative and unique way for me to become familiar with her house and get even more excited about my visit. Her hints would include the refrigerator with my favorite Kool-Aid, or the kitchen table with a brochure for the zoo or the museum, or the patio with a new kite, or the bathroom with a new bottle of bubble bath, or the counter with a box of my favorite bakery cookies, or the basement with supplies for a craft project to do together. My treasure hunt always ended under my pillow with a note telling me how happy she was that I was there.

The special connection in our family between grandparents and grandchildren has continued to our own children. Our daughters were given dolls with stories, wardrobes, furniture, and cookbooks from the same time periods in which their grandmother and great-grandmother grew up. This created a unique opportunity for them to learn in a fun way how life was different for their grandmother and great-grandmother at their age. This experience provided a lovely gift of empathy, understanding, sharing, and meaningful relationship between the generations.

Passing On a Spiritual Heritage

I (Dave) will be forever indebted to my grandmother for the spiritual heritage she passed on to me. I can remember as a boy coming downstairs in the morning and seeing Grandmother Hipp with an open Bible in her lap. I knew from an early age that she prayed for me, and from time to time she talked with me about her faith in God. I can remember when she was sick and in lots of pain, she never complained and had such a peace. As a boy, that impressed me. Often I would go to church with Grandmother, and there I got to know other kids and adults who had a strong faith. Actually, it was through Mr. Dover, one of my Sunday school teachers in my grandmother's church, that I later became a Christian. Never underestimate your influence on your grandchildren!

The Other Side

Are you wishing your children had grandparents like Dave's grandmother who had a spiritual heritage to pass down to your children, but your parents aren't religiously inclined and show no evidence of a personal relationship with God? I (Dave) can also relate. While my mom was a quiet, loving Christian, my dad was antagonistic to almost anything religious. For most of his life he had no spiritual interest and would rather not talk about God. I prayed for him and occasionally would try to initiate a conversation about deeper issues in life, but he quickly rebuffed the attempt. Quite honestly, I doubted he would ever respond spiritually.

In the last years of his life, he developed a rare form of Parkinson's disease and was in much discomfort. As his condition worsened, I made one last visit. My great desire was to see him open his heart to Christ, but it wasn't to be. I went home rather hopeless and disappointed. Within a few weeks I got

---

When I was a young boy, my grandmother offered me money to read and memorize Proverbs and Psalms. She offered me five dollars a month if I would read one proverb and five psalms a day. (You finish the books in a month if you do so!) And she offered five dollars for each psalm that I memorized. I know that child-development specialists and Christian educators argue about the wisdom of this method of education, but I can say that it worked for me! I failed to get rich from her offer, but I developed a passion for the Psalms and a deep understanding of "the ways of wisdom" that are found in Proverbs.

—John Bell

the phone call that he was in the hospital and near death. My sister and I quickly flew to Albuquerque to be with him. We both were burdened that he had rejected God all his life and prayed for one last opportunity to share with him. You can imagine our surprise when one morning as we arrived at the hospital, the nurse told us that during the night our dad had called out several times, "Holy Jesus, pray for me." This was significant, because at this stage he could rarely articulate any words or communicate verbally.

We asked him about what the nurse had told us and to blink twice if it was true. He blinked twice. Amazed, we continued, "Dad, would you like to invite Christ into your life? If you want to, just blink twice." He blinked twice! He continued to communicate with us through his eyes to the point we were convinced that he had at the last moment of his life turned to God. Later that afternoon, he went into a coma and the next day passed away peacefully in his sleep. While it's sad that he waited so long to respond spiritually, I have the comfort of knowing Dad found peace with God. I share this story to encourage you to never give up, to keep praying for your loved ones. Your faith and prayers may in the end make all the difference in the world.

A Word of Caution

We need to recognize that we come from diverse family backgrounds and like Dave's dad, not all of our parents, grandparents, or adult children may share our faith and values. While our desire is to pass on a spiritual heritage—sometimes in both directions—we need to be sensitive in the way we go about doing it. We need to respect boundaries and be sensitive in how we approach talking about faith and values.

Passing on a Spiritual Heritage—What Grandparents Can Do

- Provide the opportunity for your grandchild to attend a summer Christian camp.
- Keep a prayer diary for each grandchild.
- Read Bible and value-based stories to your grandchild.
- Possibly help with tuition for your grandchild to attend a Christian school.
- Give each grandchild a Christian book every year.

Let the Fun Begin!

With such noble challenges before us to pass on a heritage, let's consider how to foster better grandparent/grandchild relationships through focused attention.

If you are the parent or grandparent, stop and evaluate present grandparent-grandchild relationships. If these are not as close as you would like, now is the time to be intentional and plan times together. While it's great for grandparents and grandchildren to all be together, we need to be aware that relationships are built in twos, so we would encourage you to look for ways to facilitate one-on-one times. Consider the following:

Just-Me-and-You times. For a number of years, we (the Arps) resided in Vienna, Austria, and actually those were the best years of connection to grandparents for our sons. My (Claudia's) parents came to visit us once or twice a year, and we were in charge of their itinerary. Several times during their visit, I planned "Just-me-and-Grandmother" times and "Just-me-and-Grandfather" times. I would give them a list of questions and topics they might want to talk about with their grandson, and then I sent them off with each grandson, one at a time, up the street to the ice-cream shop, knowing ice cream would be a big hit with our boys.

Did my parents cooperate? Yes, but sometimes it took much effort to get them out the door. Was it worth it? Yes! Each time they would come back laughing and enjoying this unique relationship over the generational span of many years. Now that we have eight grandchildren of our own, we realize we need to make sure we are bonding with each grandchild and that we are having our own "Just-Me-and-You" times.

When we had the opportunity to work at the United Nations in Vienna, Austria, promoting parenting support groups, part of our job was to interview families from around the world who were working at the U.N. We made an amazing discovery. Most of the family and cultural traditions were being passed from the grandparents to the grandchildren—actually skipping a generation! Think about this. What traditions would you like to pass on to your grandkids?

—DAVE AND CLAUDIA

"A La Grandparent" cooking together. Cooking together is a wonderful way for grandparents and grandchildren to spend individualized time together—plus it's really a lot of fun for both. I (Claudia) have found that I do things with our grandchildren that I never would have done with our own kids—like letting the grandkids make a royal mess when we make cookies together! We have wonderful pictures of grandkids covered with flour and sprinkles. In the background you can see the kitchen that is also dusted with flour and glittering with sprinkles. With my own children, we made cookies, but not with such abandon or mess!

Games, puzzles and crafts. Look for natural interests. One grandfather always brings his grandson a puzzle when he comes for a visit. Both granddad and grandson look forward to their special time together. Another grandparent often brings craft projects to do with each grandchild when she comes to visit.

Connecting children with great-grandparents. We can also facilitate relationships between children and great-grandparents. My (Claudia's) almost 91-year-old mother discovered that she had cancer and actually died two weeks later. But in those last days she connected in a deep and special way with many of her extended family, and especially with her oldest great-granddaughter. Our sons came to say good-bye to their grandmother, affectionately called "Cattee." Each brought his oldest child, and the oldest among them was our granddaughter Sophie, who at that time was 4 years old. Sophie and her 3-year-old cousin, Hayden, each day picked wildflowers for Cattee. Their great-grandmother loved to have them bring the flowers to her in her bedroom and present them to her.

One day, during a conversation with Mother, she expressed sadness because she had always wanted to give Sophie a tea set but had never gotten around to doing it. "That's not a problem," I told her. That afternoon I went to Wal-Mart and bought a lovely tea set complete with colorful dishes, cups, saucers, and cooking utensils. I wrapped it in bright paper and pink ribbon. Then I gave it to Mother to give to Sophie.

Etched in my memory is the picture of Mother giving this gift to Sophie and the unabashed delight on Sophie's face when she opened it with her great-grandmother. Before long Sophie and Cattee were having a tea party together. Sophie made pancakes for Cattee, which she "ate" with great enthusiasm. The next day Sophie and her dad left. She never saw her great-grandmother again. I don't know if she remembers the tea party with

Cattee, but I can keep the memory alive for her in stories about her great-grandmother.

For me personally, it is a memory I shall carry forever. You see, my mom wasn't "grandkid savvy." She loved her grandchildren and great-grandchildren but didn't really understand how to connect with them. She enjoyed watching them more than really relating to them. To see her sheer joy when she entered into relationship with Sophie through their tea-party-for-two really meant a lot to me.

Watching for Pitfalls

While looking for ways to build relationships between grandparents and grandchildren, we need to mention a few pitfalls to avoid:

For the grandparent:

- Don't play favorites. Children pick up on this quickly, and it will torpedo relationships.
- Don't overstep. Remember you are the grandparent, not the parent, and respect the parents' rules and guidelines.
- Take the initiative. Don't wait for your grandchild to initiate getting together.
- Be fair.
- We know they are adorable, but please don't give preference to babies!

For parents:

- Don't just look at your parents as the "baby-sitters."
- Don't overlook spontaneous opportunities for your parent to spend individual time with your children.

Grandparent-Grandchildren Fun Tips

- Sports, hiking, and other outdoor activities—learn to hit tennis balls together, go swimming, or take a hike together.
- Weekly phone calls—Get your own toll-free number and give it to your grandchildren.
- Connect through e-mail and Web sites.
- Give your grandchildren your picture to put in their room.

- When a grandparent oversteps his or her authority, be sensitive and diplomatic when confronting him or her.
- Be sure you are giving your parents access to your children. Even if you are struggling with your relationship with your parents, don't penalize your child! Let your children spend time with their grandparents.

Helping Out

When we lived in the same town as my (Margaret's) 82-year-old grandmother, and our girls were 1 and 4, my grandmother insisted on helping one afternoon a week. This meant that she would drive her car to our house with her portable oxygen tank and baby-sit for several hours in the afternoon so that I could do errands or attend meetings unencumbered.

I remember wondering if she was baby-sitting the girls or they were baby-sitting her! Actually, the bond they formed with their great-grandmother was a strong and beautiful one. Looking back, we are all extremely grateful for her persistence and insistence on being involved in a helping manner with our family, and we miss her greatly. Our advice: Take the risk—seize the day—*carpe diem!*

The Jam Grandparent

Just as today's parents are sharing parenting responsibilities and co-parenting, grandparents are "co-grandparenting" and often help out when adult children are in a jam. Increased life expectancy and early retirement of grandfathers are among the most dramatic changes for the present generation of grandparents. Grandfathers are much more involved with their grandchildren than they were in past generations. Often they care for grandchildren and are available to help out in times of need. Jane Bell (John's mother) coined the phrase "Jam Grandparents." She points out that while many grandparents tend to be younger, less emotionally involved, and more independent, they are readily available to help their children and grandchildren when they are in a jam.

For instance, Joe picks up his granddaughter and grandson each day from school and carts them to their after-school activities while their mom is at work. Ruby flew halfway across the country to care for her two preschool grandchildren while her daughter had surgery. Lena and Ralph took their grandkids with them to Disney World while their son and daughter moved into their new home.

Adult Children and Parents

In this section, we will use the term "adult children" and "parents" rather broadly as we consider adult/parental relationships. For instance, "adult children" might also be parents or even grandparents. I (Claudia) remember my mother referring to us as "the children" even when she was 90 years old and we were no spring chickens—actually we were already grandparents. While we dislike the term "adult child"—hopefully we are no longer childish—the word "offspring" seems so technical, and it's too laborious to always say "adult son and/or adult daughter." But the parental bond is a lifelong bond with many unique challenges and is an important one to address, so for lack of a better term, when we use "adult child" we simply are referring to the younger member of the parental intergenerational relationship.

Complicated? You bet! Such difficulty in finding adequate terms to identify who we're referencing is only the tip of the iceberg. For instance, consider that many parents are also children of older parents, so they are relating on both sides—one side as a daughter or son and the other side as parents and/or grandparents. Adult parental relationships are quite complex, and how you negotiate them impacts your relationship with your in-laws and other extended-family members. So we need to consider what we can do to facilitate healthy adult/parental relationships.

One survey participant wrote: "Please don't ignore your stepgrandchildren for holidays and birthdays. Grandparents should understand that when their child marries (or even cohabits) with someone who has a child from a previous relationship, that 'step' child should be considered equal to their own biological grandchildren. There's nothing that will alienate a new in-law faster than not including their children in gift giving, family vacations, etc. If the stepgrandchild is scheduled to spend a week with the 'other' parent during a time when you are scheduling, let's say, a beach vacation, better to change the date so the stepgrandchild can be with his or her new cousins. This comes from my own bitter family experience with my in-laws, who are now estranged from my brother-in-law's family for exactly this reason, plus other slights heaped on, such as inequality in gift giving."

Understanding Adult Parental Dynamics

So many changes have occurred in the extended family so fast that it is hard to generalize anything about adult child/parent relationships. We know that all family relationships can be complicated, but factors like changes in life expectancy, early retirement, and our mobile society have greatly altered how mothers and fathers and adult children relate to one another. The challenge to develop common ground—which is automatic when families live together in the nuclear family or when grandparents live next door—is a daunting one. Some other factors include different cultural experiences, relocation and multiple moves, and divorce and remarriage. Transportation in general and the car in particular have changed how parents and adult children relate.

Add to the above what's going on in individual relationships, such as the all-too-common situations where there are past hurts—neglect, harsh words, favoritism, and so on—and relationships can get incredibly complicated! While we will address the harder issues in Challenge Six, we do want to give some general tips in this section for building better adult child/parent relationships. We also refer you to Challenge One, where we talked about the importance of forgiveness. Forgiveness is the oil that lubricates extended family relationships, and it's vital in the adult child/parent relationship. Just transitioning into adulthood is a great challenge for both parent and child and usually comes with some hurts on both sides. If not dealt with, these hurts and misunderstandings may fester for years.

A Word to the Younger Generation from the Arps

To help you better understand your parents, let us share a few of our observations. Many of your parents are members of the Silent Generation and aren't always good about expressing their feelings. They are not as self-confident or self-assured as the younger generation or as secure in their roles as were their own parents, whose culture was not as complex as our world is today.

Your parents may appear to be less emotionally involved and more independent. This may be in part because they feel overcriticized and unappreciated and are uncertain of the role they are to play in your life. Deep down they want to be involved in your life and with their grandchildren, but they may not always feel needed or just don't know how to foster a closer relationship with you. They may be more self-protective against heartache or unstable family life and as a result may choose less involvement. Our suggestion for you is to look for ways to pull them into your family and make them feel loved, appreciated, and wanted.

A Word to the Older Generation from the Bells

While at times older adults may feel overcriticized and underappreciated, your adult children and grandchildren desperately want you to be a part of their lives. The words that describe the lives of younger adult children are "busy, busy, and busy." Time is the sacred part of life that is often missing, and time at home is even rarer and more valuable. Family life in the twenty-first century is different from when older adults were children.

Consider a 24-hour slice of their life: Look at their family calendar on the refrigerator or ask to see your son's or daughter's Palm Pilot! You will see that their lives are filled with activities that were once considered extracurricular but are now considered core-curricular for most families. Single, married with no kids, or married with kids does not seem to matter. They are all scheduled tightly.

If they are married with kids, it is likely that both parents are working outside the home. If one spouse is not working, he or she is probably an over-committed, overworked, in-demand volunteer at school, church, Scouts, and the ball field. Home schooling has become quite common, and if this is the choice, then the line between home and school is completely blurred.

Most young children today participate in several after-school activities, from sports to music to computer classes to church activities. Many of those same teachers and coaches have a "no practice, no play" policy that puts a premium on making every practice and doing everything that is asked and required. And, not to be outdone, young adults also sign up for scheduled activities such as co-ed softball teams, ballet classes, church retreats, and Bible studies.

Domestically, young families are less likely than older adults to sit down together at the table for dinner. Young families eat out, pick up fast food, or grab a power bar and an energy drink when they fill up the car with gas! Weekends and evenings are often filled with never-ending home improvement projects or trips to the mall.

We suggest trying to accept that young adults live in a culture that—rightly or wrongly—keeps them very, very busy and often broke! (Savings rates have plummeted and debt has soared for them in general.) These cultural realities—such as their busy lifestyle—may not be very healthy or wise, but for the moment they are cultural givens that you may not like but cannot change. Understand that it's the culture in which your adult children live and it is hard for them to slow down.

But if you peel off the layers of the differences between your culture and theirs, underneath is your son or daughter and maybe your grandchildren who are your blood relatives. The apple doesn't generally fall too far from the tree, and remember that they are coping with their awkward age as best they can, much as you did at their age. They may be busy, but be assured that in most cases they do yearn to have you involved in their lives and want to share life with you. Respect their schedules, but look for time. Don't be afraid to try to get on their schedule. Go with them to their activities. Support their interests. Recognize that those tender moments you long for may occur in the parking lot of the ball field and not around the kitchen table.

Relating to Older Parents

Throughout life the dynamics of the adult child/parent relationship come into play. What goes around will come around! Giving due respect to our elders, let's look a little deeper at the relationship between adult children, who are often grandparents themselves, and aging parents, who may also be grandparents and great-grandparents. Actually, much of what we are getting ready to share will apply to all the ages and stages of adult parental relationships.

Barb visited her mother every day in the assisted care facility and took her favorite magazines, little goodies, and fresh flowers out of the yard. When complimented one day for her attention and care, she said, "Oh, this is very selfish of me. I want my daughters to do this for me when I am old."

This story should motivate all of us to stay in relationship and provide for aging parents, but sometimes it's not easy to do. Consider the following complicating factors or potential roadblocks that may hamper relationships with older parents/grandparents:

Lack of trust. When the generations do not trust each other, it's hard to keep relationships positive. Not all adult child/parent relationships are healthy. If you have great relationships with your parents and/or adult children, be thankful. But if lack of trust in an intergenerational relationship is present, you can do what you can, but realize that some things may never change. In such a situation, a better relationship may require that you become more independent and keep the relationship with that particular family member more distant. Good boundaries (as good fences) may help you keep the relationship manageable. (More on this in Challenge Seven.)

Unrealistic demands and manipulation. Norman, the elderly father in the movie *On Golden Pond*, in the middle of having a heart attack was asked by his wife, "Norman, how is your heart?" Norman answered, "I'm in a lot of pain; nothing for you to worry about." We chuckle because most of us understand what it feels like to be emotionally manipulated.

A survey participant wrote, "My mother-in-law is like an emotional octopus. She attaches her tentacles to me and sucks out my patience and energy. Yesterday she called and said, 'I just called to let you know I'm getting along all right so you won't worry about me.' Her real message was, 'Honey, if you really cared about me you would have called first to see how I am.'"

On the other hand is the mother who values her independence but whose son keeps calling and checking on her. He tries to manipulate her by telling her continually that she is aging and insisting that he help her with her finances even thought she is capable of handling her own affairs. He's slowly chipping away at her self-confidence. After all, he assumes that as his mother ages, he is to become the parent. She thinks otherwise.

Dealing with Demands and Manipulation

Establish clear boundaries and stand your ground when dealing with a demanding or manipulative relative. For example, you might say, "I know you want all of us to be together for Thanksgiving so you can get your annual Christmas card picture of the grandchildren, but we do not think it is fair to spend every Thanksgiving with you to the exclusion of the other side of the family. We will alternate holiday celebrations with each side of our family." In Challenge Seven we'll take a closer look at how boundary setting can help you deal with demands and manipulation.

Keep your marriage and your nuclear family the first priority before dealing with extended-family demands. This may mean assuring your spouse that you will not disappear to the golf course or the shopping mall or the gym—leaving him or her to deal with your family alone for extended periods of time. Or, assuring your children that even though they are several years older or younger than the other children present, they are not expected to automatically baby-sit or be baby-sat by the others.

Be prepared to sacrifice. If part of the manipulation you must deal with includes financial strings, you may need to make the decision to sacrifice. The cartoon where the husband says to his wife, "Great news, honey—my parents said that we don't have to come for Thanksgiving this year—they will simply write us out of the will!" humorously illustrates this principle.

Give and take—also known as compromise. Remember the saying "Company, like fish, smells after three days!" Keep your visits or the visits of family members short, sweet, and successful. Granted, this is not always possible when you must travel great distances to visit one another. You can, however, plan for time apart within an extended visit and keep the relationship the priority.

Building Positive Bridges

We all desire to have positive relationship with our parents. Here are some practical ways to keep a positive connection.

Record Family History. Given today's technology with digital cameras and videos, it's easy to record family history. We (Dave and Claudia) have an ancient slide show that our sons put together for Father's Day years ago. Our challenge now is to transfer our slide show to DVD or other media to preserve our family history.

Family history can pull in the whole family gang and can promote hours

---

Tips for Relating to Aging Parents

- Do unto your parents as you would have your children do unto you!
- Respect your parents' desire to control their own lives.
- Tactfully initiate conversations about car keys, nursing homes, medical coverage, and so on. Recognize that these conversations may include some anger and tears.
- Together, you may want to consult a member of the clergy about funeral plans.
- Remember, you won't get a second chance to do this.

—JOHN AND MARGARET

of great family interaction. An interesting activity is to make a list of family sayings—those quips that are passed down, like, "I was just born too soon" or "You're as cute as an India rubber bouncing ball"—that help us appreciate our unique family heritage.

Send pictures. We've already talked about how easy it is today to send digital pictures via e-mail and the Internet. Elderly parents may prefer an old-fashioned scrapbook. During the years we (the Arps) lived in Austria, we often sent scrapbooks for Christmas presents to our parents and to Dave's grandmother. It was a great way to keep them in touch with our family.

Do something out of the ordinary. When we visited Dave's family we rarely ate out, so for his dad's eighty-fourth birthday we suggested taking him out to eat. We were surprised when he enthusiastically said yes. We took him to an old, well-known restaurant that he had never been to even though he had lived in the same city for 30 years. We had a delightful meal, one he talked about for a long time.[2]

Relating to Adult Children

Certainly, when we're old we all want to have good relationships with our children and extended family. How can we help bring this about? First, we must make sure we have moved past the adolescent struggles of days gone by and redefine relationships on an adult level. Parents must let their children go and reconnect on an adult level. Children must assume adult responsibilities and see themselves as an independent unit—being mature and realizing their parents owe them nothing!

Closely tied to claiming adult status is recognizing boundaries when adult children marry. "As parents we promise to stand beside, not between." That's a line from the wedding ceremony of one of the Arp sons, the line that is most prominent in our memory. Remembering it is one thing; actually doing it, however, is another! Easy or not, it's the key to being a great parent and parent-in-law.

Letting go is being willing to take a lower priority in your son's or daughter's life. Your part is to play second fiddle, and that's okay. A significant problem in marriages, not only in America but all over the world, is the failure of parents to let go. This may be particularly difficult if you are close to your child. It's not easy to stand beside and encourage your children to make it their first priority to please their spouse rather than mom and dad. The key is letting go emotionally, which goes much deeper than physically distancing yourself.

Facilitate Serendipitous Moments

Serendipitous moments do not have to be expensive or big—it is the surprise element that makes the moment memorable. You might try a trip to Dairy Queen for ice cream or Starbucks for coffee, or a handwritten note in the mail containing words of encouragement and support, or a homemade cake or casserole, or even a phone call expressing love and assurance of prayers on another's behalf.

At rare times, serendipitous moments might be extravagant. One such moment came our (John and Margaret's) way one year early in our marriage. John was asked to be in a dear childhood friend's wedding near New York City. At the time, our budget was limited, our children were 2 and 5, and we had not gotten away by ourselves in quite some time. John's parents generously gave us the use of their car, offered to keep the girls while we were away, and paid for an over-the-top two-day stay after the wedding at one of the finest hotels New York City has to offer. In fact, they insisted that we stop on the way in Hershey, Pennsylvania, at the Hershey Hotel, where they had stayed years ago and enjoyed it immensely. It was a fabulous trip—one of our all-time favorites—and a totally unexpected, serendipitous gift.

ADULT SIBLINGS AND SPOUSES

Fostering positive relationships among siblings (including their spouses) is one of the most daunting challenges of the extended family. We must admit, we haven't heard an abundance of success stories. Certainly, fostering healthy relationships requires a big dose of tolerance and acceptance. At times it will involve identifying stress points in the relationship and dealing with them.

Problems with siblings go all the way back to Cain and Abel. Sibling rivalry, even if not a problem in the growing-up years, often surfaces when siblings marry and have children. Competition and comparison run rampant.

We (Dave and Claudia) remember sitting in a restaurant with our boys, then ages 3, 7, and 9, who were needling one another—basically being pills—and watching two young men who were brothers interacting at another table. Matthias and Cass were in their twenties and were obviously connecting, their laughter evidence that they really enjoyed being together. We had been around Matthias and Cass several other times, and their close relationship as adult siblings always intrigued us. We talked about how we hoped that someday when our sons were grown, they would have as close and positive a relationship as Matthias and Cass. Other parents express a similar desire. Perhaps you do too. What can we, as parents, do to help facilitate healthy relationships for the future?

We've learned that if we want our adult sons and daughters-in-law to be friends, we need to help them get together and allow them time alone when the whole family gathers. Face it, when they are alone together, the dynamics are different. They can open up and share more deeply with one another.

Recently, we (John and Margaret) invited John's sister and her husband and their boys to visit us, and were thrilled when they accepted and actually came! It was the first time in our memory that we had been alone with just their family and ours. This was a unique opportunity to relate on a different level, and we felt so much more relaxed and easygoing than when all of the family is together. We are hoping to have the same opportunity with our other adult siblings and their families.

Sisters-in-Law Out on the Town
Traditionally, our (John and Margaret's) families have gathered at John's parents' mountain home in early August for some extended-family together time. One year, my mother-in-law heard that a famous and well-loved author

---

Believe it or not, our girls do not always get along like angels! When this occurs, I pull out my most serious weapon—the sister factor. I never had a sister and always wanted one (even though I am crazy about my brother), and I remind them in my most serious tone of voice that they are and always will be sisters for the rest of their lives. Friends may come and go, but sisters are sisters for life. I guess time will tell if this has been a successful strategy. If nothing else, it joins them in their contempt and disdain at having to hear the same speech again from their mother!

—MARGARET BELL

was going to be in town doing a flower arranging and table decorations seminar. Knowing that both my sister-in-law and I love to entertain, my mother-in-law purchased two tickets to the event and offered to keep all four grandchildren so we could attend together. I distinctly recall that wonderful feeling of freedom as the two of us drove out of the driveway for a day of unfettered fun.

SIBLING RIVALRY

Every family with more than one child must deal with sibling rivalry at some point in their family journey. For some the rivalry exists far beyond childhood and permeates their relationship as adults, and for others there may be some past experience of hurt stemming from a sibling rivalry and lingering hard feelings. Remember that though we are created in God's image, like snowflakes we are truly unique. No two of us are the same—not even "identical" twins! Translated, this means by our very nature we relate differently and are related to differently.

However, there are times when the differences in relating appear to one sibling or the other to be unjust. For example, the younger sibling receives all hand-me-down clothes from the older sibling. Or the younger sibling is allowed certain privileges at a younger age than the older sibling was allowed to experience them. Or one sibling's children are treated differently by the grandparents than the other sibling's children. Often parents or grandparents may be totally unaware of the perceived injustice, and hurt feelings may fester.

Nowhere is clear communication needed more than when addressing the issue of sibling rivalry with a sibling or parent. Without being confrontational, try to share your deepest feelings. This is best done by using "I" statements (e.g., "I don't know if you realize that allowing Hayley to pierce her ears when she was 10 while I had to wait until I was 13 still really bothers me," or "I feel hurt that you will baby-sit Jan's children overnight but you won't keep our children overnight"). Opening the door to honest, nonconfrontational communication can help to begin the process of resolving past hurts and lingering rivalry issues when everyone seeks to understand and be understood.

Of course, some sibling breaches are quite serious and may require more than clear communication. We all know those sad stories about brothers and sisters who haven't spoken in years. In those cases, one person must make an intentional decision to seek to restore the relationship and begin the arduous process of reconciliation. This brave person must generally swallow pride, take initiative to make the contact, and extend or seek forgiveness—depending on what initially caused the rift.

As we said earlier, forgiveness is the oil that lubricates family relationships, and nowhere is it more needed than among siblings. If you are struggling with being willing to forgive a sibling, please reread the section on forgiving your relatives in Challenge One.

The Cousins, Aunts, and Uncles

The best way to facilitate connecting with cousins, aunts, and uncles is to spend time together. When we asked our daughters what would help them know their cousins better, one daughter answered, "Actually living close together!" While at the present that isn't an option, we do look for ways to get together and stay connected.

In my (Margaret's) family of origin, we had several family reunions. My father is the youngest of four boys and I have nine cousins—seven boys and two girls. I am not sure the adults were intentional about literally turning us all loose in a basement playroom or a backyard or even a park across the street to entertain ourselves while they visited, but it was what I remember as being the most fun times with my cousins.

Now, with our own children, it seems like this is a good way to allow them to develop their own friendships with their cousins. When left to their

One clever grandmother came up with a creative plan for fostering positive relationships between cousins. She invited three grandkids from different families to come for a visit. This was a major financial investment as she flew kids from California to Michigan. She said it was a great way for the cousins to get to know one another. From year to year she would invite different grandkids but was careful to make sure all felt included and that she wasn't "playing favorites."

own devices, they are quite creative and come up with the most fascinating games in which all choose their own part. In fact, I would not be totally surprised to see our 16-year-old slip back into her role of restaurant hostess while her 14-year-old boy cousin and 13-year-old sister resume their chef roles—complete with aprons and hats—and the 10-year-old cousin reverts to the difficult-to-please customer!

Family get-togethers give the children an opportunity to get to know their aunts and uncles—and perhaps see a side of them they wouldn't discover through phone calls and letters. One night after dinner on an extended family vacation, we (the Bell clan) were all tired and ready for bed. Some were already bathed and in their pajamas. The dishes from dinner were not yet done. One uncle announced that he was not tired and not ready to go to bed and did not want to do the dishes. "What do you want to do? It's late!" we asked.

"I want to go ride go-carts!" he declared with wide eyes. Soon we were all in cars heading to the go-cart track—even though none of us had ever been go-carting before! We raced cars until the track closed; then we went to Dairy Queen until *it* closed. Finally, we fell into bed at 1:00 A.M. The aunts, uncles, and cousins will never forget it. Bravo!

CONNECTING WITH IN-LAWS

Connecting with in-laws is a two-way street. You want to connect with your new in-laws whether you are the son- or daughter-in-law or the parents-in-law. Our (Dave and Claudia) parents knew each other before we ever met. I (Claudia) remember telling my dad that I had a date with Dave Arp. His comment fascinated me: "If he's anything like his mother, he's really nice!"

Take the Initiative
Look for ways to get to know your in-law's extended family. Our lives have been enriched by getting to know the parents of our daughters-in-law. It's great if you can meet and get to know your in-law's family, but it's not always easy to achieve. Maybe you live in California and your in-laws live in Maine. Visiting each other may not be feasible, but you can stay in touch through the telephone, e-mail and the post office. If it is possible to visit, it can be fun to see where your son- or daughter-in-law grew up and to look through

family scrapbooks. Times like these help you to connect and appreciate the unique past that influenced the wonderful person your child's spouse is today.

Jennifer shared with us the frustration she felt as a young mom trying to balance visits with two sets of parents who lived just a few minutes apart. The parents did not have much in common except expecting Jennifer and her family to spend priority time with them. However they tried to work it out, no one was pleased. Perhaps if the parents had put forth more effort in building a relationship with one another, it would have been easier for Jennifer to find balance.

But what can Jennifer do? She needs to clearly communicate to both sets of parents what she and her family can and cannot do. We would suggest inviting the parents for dinner together and talking to them at the same time. A shared meal can help bring about an open discussion. You are giving the nonverbal message, "I care about you. You're important to me, so I have prepared a special meal for you."

Over dinner, Jennifer and her husband might raise the issue of times together and express their frustration over wanting to spend priority time with each set of parents yet finding it stressful to always have to get together separately. As a result of this discussion, their parents might agree to have one time a month when they all get together.

Ways to Show Acceptance to Your Son- or Daughter-in-Law

- Never criticize the way your son-in-law dresses or your daughter-in-law wears her makeup. One mother-in-law put it this way: "Only look at their eyes. That's all that counts."
- Watch the nonverbal communication! It's easy to criticize without saying a word. We all know "the look"!
- Whatever you spend on gifts for your own adult child, spend an equivalent on your in-law.
- Keep them up-to-date on your family's activities.
- Give a compliment instead of a critique.

—DAVE AND CLAUDIA

So many times we try to deal with frustrating situations while we are caught up in the stresses—like when both parents are demanding our time with them at the same time. If we can share our frustrations with our parents at another time (between events when we aren't as stressed), it's more likely that we will find creative solutions.

Feeling Included

No one wants to be on the outside looking in, but it's easy for an in-law to feel that way. One reason you might feel left out is simply not knowing the other in-laws' family history. Several years ago while we (Dave and Claudia) were visiting Dave's parents, his mom pulled out all the old boxes of pictures, newspaper clippings, and family history. We had a ball looking through the Arp history. I loved all the cute pictures of Dave as a little boy, but what really fascinated me were the pictures and articles about his mom, Lillian.

I could visualize her as the young mother of two little children and could almost feel her love and devotion to her family. Being a military family, they lived all over the world. I imagined how she provided the stability and emotional comfort for her family's many transitions. It gave me a new appreciation and love for this lady who so influenced the one person I love more than anyone else in the whole world!

Remember That You Have at Least One Thing in Common

What if you feel you have little in common with your in-laws? Listen to this story. Recently I (Claudia) attended a bridal luncheon for the daughter of a good friend. After a delicious brunch, each guest was asked to give the bride one tip for getting along with her future mother-in-law. Since we were in the process of researching this book, I wanted to say something really profound, but the one thing that stood out in my mind was this tip: "Remember, you will always have one thing in common—you both love the same person." This advice can be a great help when there are many other areas where you disagree.

One survey participant wrote how she tried for 20 years to relate to her mother-in-law but never felt accepted or respected. But then her mother-in-law finally began to come around, and today they have a pleasant relationship. If you are struggling with an in-law who is totally different from you, you can help build mutual respect by remembering what you do have in common—you both love the same person. Whatever your differences, let us encourage you to concentrate on what you have in common, not on areas where you disagree. (Hopefully, it won't take 20 years to build a relationship!) You may be surprised by what you find.

It's your choice. You can concentrate on the positive things you see in your in-law, or you can dwell on the negative. You may even admire some of the ways he or she is totally different from you. Each person is unique, and it's up to you to appreciate that uniqueness. Here are some ways to camp on the positive:

- Compliment your in-law in the presence of others.
- Make a list of your in-law's positive qualities.
- List the ways you are different that give variety to your family tree.
- Affirm your in-law. Is he or she taking a risk to grow in an area—maybe learning a new sport, trying low-fat cooking, or working out? Is your in-law bravely switching jobs or professions to something better suited and more fulfilling? Look for opportunities to give some encouragement.

OTHER GENERAL RELATIONSHIP-BUILDING TIPS

Building relationships with extended family is more of an art than a science. But we do have several closing suggestions to help foster better relationships. Consider the following:

Relating to Your Mother/Father-in-Law

- Call just to say hello—have no agenda and keep the phone call short.
- Take the initiative to apologize and to forgive your mother/father-in-law if needed.
- Write a letter and mention those things you appreciate about her/him.
- Avoid all forms of manipulation.
- Try to see things from your in-law's perspective.
- Do what you can to facilitate a positive relationship, but don't assume responsibility for her/his happiness.

—JOHN AND MARGARET

Spend one-on-one time together. Relationships are built in twos, so whether it's a parent, sibling, aunt, uncle, cousin, grandparent, or in-law, look for ways to spend some time alone together.

Facilitate times together. Encourage other family members to spend time together. Perhaps you can encourage two families to get together without everyone else being there. Siblings, for instance, need to spend some quality time together, and that's hard to do when the whole clan is present.

Meet at a neutral site. With siblings and cousins this is often helpful. Even when the grandparents are present, being in a neutral setting will change the dynamics. No one has to be the host and all can participate equally.

If teenagers are involved, let them bring a friend. One 15-year-old said, "Vacation time is time to relax with my friends, so I'd have more fun if I could take a friend along on our family get-together."

Keep your sense of humor. Nowhere is the ability to laugh more important than when the extended family gets together. Remember to laugh at yourself and with each other!

Acknowledge that some families are closer than others. If you live in the same town with your extended family, it is natural that you will do more with and for those who live close by. Remember to have realistic expectations, and realize that some families are just closer to one another than are other families.

Be flexible. When you're with the extended family, don't always insist that your nuclear family rules be enforced, unless health or moral issues are at stake. Oreos every day for a week won't hurt unless a child is obese or has diabetes.

For years, whenever we visited Dave's parents, I (Claudia) could always count on finding candy corn on a certain shelf in the kitchen. That's one thing Lillian and I had in common—our sweet tooth. The candy corn was a simple act of thoughtfulness but one I still remember years later. Think about your own son- or daughter-in-law. Do you know one or two things that would make him or her feel at home? Buy a favorite cereal, flavored coffee or tea, or vegetarian specialty. Have fresh flowers in the bedroom. You can even put a chocolate candy kiss on each pillow.

Remember that good relationships are in the eyes of the beholder. Do what you can to foster positive relationships, and be thankful for those times when everyone gets along. Remember, in the end it's the relationship that really counts!

Challenge Six

Facing the Hard Issues

Let us now turn our attention to some of the more difficult issues that tend to hamper harmony in extended families. These are what we call "the hard issues." These are the situations that keep us awake at night—that put worry lines on our faces. They raise questions that often have no answer—certainly no easy answer.

The hard issues are the source of most major tension in extended-family relationships and generally deal with values—religious, cultural, ethical, and generational. Differences over these inevitably cause clashes in extended-family relationships. For the Scott family, tension runs high when Sean visits with Rafael and when making sleeping arrangements for Hayley and Bill, who are not yet married. Also, religious differences and church preferences add some strain.

The Scotts are not alone in facing hard issues. Our survey was filled with lots of painful snippets. Many of the stories we received broke our hearts. Here are a few responses to the question "What are the major sources of tension in your family?"

- "My husband's parents are both alcoholics."
- "Our 25-year-old daughter 'boomeranged' home last year into our empty nest."

- "My wife's mother was recently widowed and has become a burden."
- "My brother-in-law is a drug addict with multiple marriages."
- "How do you survive infidelity of a repentant spouse?"
- "We would like our daughter to marry her daughter's father."
- "How can you leave behind the dysfunction of the family you grew up in and still be able to have a relationship with them?"
- "How do you deal with divorced family members visiting at the same time?"
- "Why must the children act as the adults when the parents act like children?"
- "I was abused by my uncle as a child."

Here's a list of some other issues that we consider to be very hard:

- *Marital discord (that is, divorce and/or infidelity).* Although, sadly, divorce has become quite common in the modern world, it is still painful, affecting not just one couple or one family but numerous relationships, which become strained or shattered.
- *Religious differences.* Without question, for most Christians relating to family members of a different religion is a great challenge. For many who responded to our survey, this was their greatest challenge.
- *Value/ethical clashes.* People have different values on things such as pre-marital sex, abortion, divorce, homosexuality, and alcohol use. These value differences inevitably cause clashes in extended-family relationships.
- *Abuse.* Some families are absolutely torn apart by an incident of sexual or physical abuse, while many other families struggle with verbally abusive personalities. It is quite common for families to have one or more members who are constantly making insensitive remarks that hurt others. This person is often dismissed as The Jerk, but he or she can easily ruin a family gathering and make life difficult for all.
- *Homosexuality.* Few families today are equipped to deal in a healthy fashion with this very emotional issue that continues to divide American society. When a family member "comes out of the closet," many family members run for the closet, choosing to avoid the issue.
- *Alcohol/Drug Abuse.* Not only can family gatherings be ruined by one night of excessive behavior, but families that are forced to handle a substance abuser on a regular basis have a number of hard issues to deal with.

- *Financial manipulation.* Perhaps your family has one or more persons who are continually in desperate need of funds, or perhaps you have someone who continually tries to influence others with the promise of financial assistance. Money issues are tough.
- *Legal problems.* Like financially troubled family members, a relative who is facing criminal or civic legal difficulties can tear up a family.
- *Childbearing.* A number of very hard issues can surround the birth of children—unwed pregnancies, unplanned pregnancies, abortion, miscarriages, and infertility. Any of these can spiritually and psychologically devastate an extended family.
- *Aging parents.* Eventually, your parents may become dependent on you. At what point do you insist that your parent stop driving or question if he or she should stop living independently? When do parents need help making financial decisions? There are no easy answers here.
- *Estranged relatives.* Many tears have been shed at extended-family gatherings over those persons who have rejected the family or who have simply disappeared.
- *Medical issues.* Medical difficulties can be hard on extended families, especially when there is disagreement regarding the seriousness of an illness or the prescribed path to health. (Note: It seems to us that many extended families have great difficulty recognizing and learning to deal with mental illness in particular.)

This list is long and, sadly, incomplete. Some hard issues are not so easy to identify but may be equally difficult. One survey participant claims that the biggest tension in her family is her mother's overt favoritism. She writes that her mother bestows far more affection and time on her sister than on her, because she is a Christian and her mother and sister are not. Family get-togethers tend to be shallow, superficial affairs. This woman obviously faces a difficult problem: how to cling to both her faith and her extended family when they seem to be pulling her in opposite directions. Again, there is no easy solution here, and this woman is faced with a tension with which she must learn to live. It would be unwise to turn her back on her own family and lose her opportunity to witness to the love, joy, hope, and peace that her faith in Christ provides.

Your family may struggle with one or more of the issues listed above, or you may have a list of your own unique, hard-to-see, painful problems. What these issues have in common is that they all extract a heavy emotional toll from family members and that no solution is quick, easy, or obvious. Win-win is tough to find here. These are problems that generally developed over a long period of time and will need a long period of time to solve—if a solution can even be found. You can't solve in one day what took years to develop. Also, you probably will have limited control over these familial issues even though they seem to control you.

Our hope is that by dealing with some of these difficult issues, we can encourage understanding among the generations. For the younger generation, we ask you to be tolerant of your older relatives; for the older generation, we ask that you respect the younger one. All need to seek to maintain relationships with those with whom you differ.

A grandmother in our survey wrote, "Respect the fact that the younger generation is different from you. Allow them their life choices. Don't judge them by your personal standards. Recognize that they have a right to their views, and so do you." We are not sure what this grandmother meant by "personal standards." Was she talking about standards of how clean you keep your home or social courtesies of expressing thanks when a gift has been given? What if instead you are dealing with perceived violations of biblical standards? Is it possible or wise to remain nonjudgmental? For instance, what would you say and do if you felt a family member's pending divorce was unbiblical? Or what if your unmarried son or daughter were living with a partner or abusing drugs? Certainly you wouldn't just say, "Hey, you have a right to your views, and I also have a right to mine."

So, how can you keep loving and maintaining a relationship while not condoning immoral actions? If you say nothing and register no concern, won't that be perceived as condoning the behavior? But if you say something, no matter how gently, won't that likely be perceived as condemning? How can you express your concerns in a way that will not be perceived as judgmental? We suggest by choosing your words very, very carefully. You might want to review Challenge Two and Challenge Three, where we talked about how to speak the truth in love and to talk productively when we disagree.

Lynn is concerned about her son, Jason, who recently moved in with his girlfriend. Lynn believes in abstinence before marriage and is disappointed in Jason's choice. As a mom, she is hurting and feels like a failure. Should she just keep quiet, or should she share her concerns with Jason? Here's what she told us: "I try to let him know that I accept him and love him unconditionally, but I also tell him that I don't condone their living together. When they come to visit me, I provide separate rooms for them. So far they have respected my request. I can't dictate what they do when they stay in other places, but I can love them without allowing them to sleep together in my house. I do pray for Jason and for his girlfriend. I have found the book *The Power of a Praying Parent* to be a great comfort to me."

Note: Dealing with hard issues isn't always the older family member concerned about the younger family member. Many adult children are just as concerned about their parents' choices!

NO POPULARITY CONTEST!

Some parents today have the idea that the most important thing is to be liked by their adult children and other family members. If their children don't like them all the time or don't always agree with them, they assume they have been bad parents. Sometimes in a desire to be liked, they go beyond their comfort zone and then feel they have compromised their values and standards.

We are reminded of the father in *Fiddler on the Roof*. His daughter wanted to marry outside his faith, and this was just beyond what he could accept. Life is hard, and sometimes all we have are hard choices. You cannot change who you are. It is okay to hold to your standards, but allow others in your family to make their own choices. Above all, hold fast to your trust in God and pray diligently for loved ones you are concerned for.

In some cases, you will want to read and research more deeply on a particular issue or seek professional help. We encourage you to talk to your pastor or a qualified counselor. But in all cases we believe that you will need divine assistance and spiritual maturity to find the "peace of God, which transcends all understanding" that the Christian faith promises (Philippians 4:7). Here, you will need to rely on what 12-step groups usually refer to as a "Higher Power"—whom we, of course, know to be the God and Father of our Lord Jesus Christ. When you are confronted with these hard issues, we suggest you spend a lot of time on your knees in prayer. Remember that you can do all things through God in Jesus Christ who provides the necessary power to live this life, and that nothing in all of creation—not even your own extended family—can separate you from the love of God! But at the same time, do all you can to love, accept, and stay in relationship with your loved ones. Let's look closer at a few of these hard issues.

DIVORCE AND INFIDELITY

Broken marriages often result in broken extended-family relationships. Today it is unusual to find an extended family not touched by divorce or infidelity. Jim Smoke, founder of the Divorce Recovery Workshop, says that divorce is like a death with a living corpse. Though no longer married, one must keep relating to that other person as issues come up with children, finances, and extended family. Long after the divorce, feelings of failure and unforgiveness can poison family relationships.

A wife in our survey wrote, "My husband and I suspect that his divorce from his adulterous, non-Christian first wife is an unspoken tension on his family's side. Is it the shame? His mother is rude and acts like I don't exist." This mother needs to be willing to accept what life has brought to her and look for ways to go on with life and build a positive relationship with her new daughter-in-law. It's easy to get stuck and just as easy for the root of bitterness and feelings of failure to overshadow reality.[1]

Accepting a new spouse into the family can be challenging, but now let's look at how to be supportive to your own adult child, sibling—or even parent—who is divorcing, and also at what you can do to give support to children of the divorce.

Relating to the New Spouse After Divorce

- Look for ways to include the new spouse in your extended family.
- Remove pictures of the first wife or husband during visits.
- Display their picture.
- Resist talking about the former spouse in front of the new one!
- Spend some one-on-one time with the new spouse and really try to build a positive relationship.

When Your Adult Child Divorces

When an adult child divorces, how can you also be supportive of your child and grandchildren? You may feel guilty, angry, fearful, and insecure about what is happening and how life is going to change, but you don't want to dump your negative feelings on your child who is going through a divorce. There is the danger of being cut off from your child if he or she feels you are interfering. So how can you be supportive? Consider the following suggestions: (These also apply if you are dealing with the divorce of a parent or sibling.)

What you can do to support your divorcing child:

- Be a good listener. Find another way to vent your own feelings; resist bringing your feelings into conversation with your child.
- Be empathetic. Respond with, "That's difficult." "I see." "I'm sorry." Show that you care by practicing reflective listening.
- Don't give advice unless asked directly, and even then weigh your words carefully. The exception would be if any violence is involved.
- Don't be judgmental. If they get back together, your child will remember your negative statements, even if he or she is making them too. So don't say, "You're right, he's an inconsiderate bum." If you do, your child may never forgive you.
- Don't get involved in the financial end—like hiring a lawyer or advising how possessions should be divided. (In some unique situations you may need to help financially, but what we are saying is, don't try to solve it with money.)
- Be faithful with your love and support.

What your grandchild needs when parents are divorcing:

- They need you to stay in touch. You may be the only constant in their lives, and you can help them get through it.
- Reassure them that family continues and together you can overcome obstacles.
- Attend their school and sports functions.
- If your grandchild lives some distance away, keep in touch through phone calls, letters, and pictures.

What you can do after the divorce:

- Don't condemn your child: "If only you had been more attentive, he wouldn't have left." "You just spent too many hours at work and not enough at home."

- Discuss practical ways you can help, such as with day-to-day household responsibilities, or, if warranted, financially.
- Offer to help with the care of children.

Are Former In-Laws Still Family After Divorce?

After a divorce, is one still part of a former spouse's extended family? That's a good question, and the answer depends on whom you ask. In some families, the "D" word is never mentioned. Life goes on as if the ex-spouse had never existed. The divorced spouse is exiled; all relationships are severed. Of course this is harder to do if children are involved, but sometimes it still happens—with negative results.

In other situations, relationships continue. Consider Nancy's story: "My mother died during the first year of my marriage. It was a very difficult time, and my mother-in-law was incredible. We became very close and were almost like mother and daughter. We argued with each other. We were real. She was very supportive but never said, 'This is what you need to do.'

"Fast forward four years and two babies. Our second child was born with serious problems. My husband had a hard time with the whole situation and left, and I was devastated. Thank goodness, my mother-in-law stood by me. I don't know what I would have done without her."

When Nancy's marriage fell apart, her mother-in-law remained supportive and helpful. Nancy needed to go to work to support her family. In no way did Nancy's closet resemble a working woman's wardrobe, so her mother-in-law took her shopping and bought her an attractive business outfit. She stood by Nancy through the terminal illness of her 2-year-old daughter. And in the months afterward, she was thoughtful in many ways, once sending flowers with a note saying, "I know how you feel. I miss her too."

In a similar situation, could you be as supportive? Admittedly, the end of a marriage is a difficult situation, and you will have to be sensitive to your own son or daughter. You will need to respect his or her wishes as well. Strive to find the balance.

Another mother-in-law's son was killed tragically in a car accident. In spite of her own suffering, she went out and bought an expensive jacket that she knew her son was going to buy for his wife's birthday. She sent it to her daughter-in-law with a card saying, "This is something Bob would have wanted you to have."

CAN STEPFAMILIES BLEND?

Some of the hard issues revealed by our survey dealt with blended families that didn't blend so well. Dick Dunn, author of *Willing to Try Again*, says that to truly blend a family is difficult, if not impossible.

One survey participant wrote, "My mother-in-law has not accepted my children from my first marriage, and now everyone is old enough to experience her rejection. I try to explain to the kids that her rejection is not directly related to them, and if we continue to be loving, they cannot say we have been rude. My mother-in-law only calls when she needs something. Also, we are expected to be there for all holiday events. How can families connect who come together after divorce and remarriage?"

One might assume that when divorce occurs later in life and the children are older, it's easier to incorporate them into a new family situation. Not necessarily! When Dick remarried, his children were older. He assumed it would be easier at that point but later discovered that to the contrary, it was still hard. He told us about the time his college-age daughter came to visit. He was thrilled to be with her, and each evening they would go out together. He always invited his new wife, but she declined. Then one evening, as he and his daughter were leaving for dinner and a movie, his wife told him, "When you get home, I won't be here."

His wife got his attention, and they were able to regroup and get their relationship back on track. But even if children get along with the new spouse and stepsiblings, other issues confuse extended stepfamily relationships.

Relating to Stepchildren and Stepgrandchildren

- Don't show favorites!
- When giving gifts, give gifts of similar value.
- Plan one-on-one times to get to know the new family members.
- Include them in family conversations.
- Send a card or note from time to time to let them know you care.

"MOM, DAD, I'M GAY"

For parents, one of the most jolting statements they could ever hear may be the words, "Mom, Dad, I'm gay." Barbara LeBey, in her book *Family Estrangements*, writes, "For parents who subscribe to certain orthodox views of the three major religions, homosexuality is more than just a sexual deviation—it is outright sinful behavior, a sin against God."[2] For many parents, the recognition that a child is gay may present a host of questions and challenges. Few families in America today are equipped to deal with such challenges.

What goes on in parents' minds when they hear this announcement from their own child? LeBey suggests that parents may feel grief, guilt, hurt, and anxiety. They may mourn the loss of hopes, dreams, and expectations for a traditional life for their child, as well as their desires for grandchildren. They may hold themselves responsible—they might think they must have done something terribly wrong in parenting their child. And they really don't know how to respond.

While in this book we are limited in what help we might offer on this subject, we do suggest that if you are dealing with this issue in your family, you seek more in-depth help. Initially, you might want to speak with your pastor or a trained counselor. You might read *Someone I Love Is Gay: How Family & Friends Can Respond,* by Anita Worthen and Bob Davies. Focus on the Family also offers hope and encouragement through its Love Won Out conferences and other helpful resources.[3]

We suggest that you try to follow the example of Jesus and seek to give unconditional love to your son or daughter. Can you say to your child, "You are my child, and I love you no matter what"? First and foremost, your child needs to know that your love will not waver.

Whatever you do, we suggest that you try to keep your cool and resist making statements that you will later regret. Condemnatory remarks simply create estrangement and broken relationships. We encourage you to be as loving as you can. This does not mean that you approve of or accept the gay lifestyle, but it does mean that you still care.

Then, we encourage you to talk with your gay child in a loving and nonconfrontational way, sharing your concerns openly and honestly. Discuss the increased health risks he or she may face by embracing that lifestyle. Share your sorrow about the loss of potential grandchildren. Be prepared, though: Your gay son or daughter will most likely not agree with your concerns.

Sean and Rafael

Like many other families, the Scotts face the issue of the gay lifestyle with their son Sean. Tension runs high when Sean visits—especially when he visits with his male friend Rafael. Everyone wonders about their relationship. No one knows whether they are gay or not, but everyone is afraid to bring up the subject for fear that a severe argument will erupt. Although there are many private conversations on the subject, there are no public ones. No one ever asks Sean or speaks about the issue in his presence. They all love Sean, but they are worried about some of the decisions that he has made. However, they are afraid he will run off if challenged, so they continue in unhealthy denial.

While the Scotts deal with this issue by acting as if it doesn't exist, another family took a different approach. Tom and Betty's son, Justin, who was gay, wanted to bring his friend home with him for their Christmas celebration, where they were to exchange Christmas gifts. In the past, Tom and Betty had tried to take a civil approach and had been friendly and cordial to Justin's friend when they were all together. Now, their dilemma was what they should do about Christmas gifts. If they gave Justin's friend a gift, they felt that would signify that they acknowledged him as a family member. They wanted to maintain a good relationship with both Justin and his friend, but to them homosexuality was a moral issue and one they did not condone. In the end, they decided not to give him a gift, but they welcomed him into their home and were pleasant and kind.

What would you have done? Some might not have included Justin's friend in the celebration. Others might have given him a gift and treated him as a family member. Still others might have asked their son not to come. Again, the goal is to be as loving as you can, and we also recommend the book by Worthen and Davies for a fuller discussion of this tough issue.

COHABITING AND ISSUES OF SEXUALITY

Today almost 50 percent of couples cohabit before marriage. This is radically different from when we (David and Claudia) married years ago, and this is a huge issue for Christian parents, including the Scotts, who would prefer that their children wait until marriage to begin a sexual relationship.

Paul and Gloria are concerned over sleeping arrangements for Hayley and Bill. The two are engaged, but they are not yet married. Hayley's parents do not think they should sleep together until they are married; others in the family disagree. The older grandchildren are watching eagerly to see how the discussion goes and what the decision will be, but sadly the discussion never happens—*at least not openly!* Tension continues to swirl around the subject. A lot of manipulation, hypocrisy, and deceit occurs. A healthy, clear discussion about sexual ethics and the importance of marriage never happens, and an actual decision is never made. This particular issue will technically be over when Bill and Hayley marry, but the hurts that may develop now could linger for years, and the patterns that are set now can ripple down through the generations that follow.

While the Scotts have absolutely no control over whether Hayley and Bill sleep together before marriage, they could initiate a conversation with Hayley and express their concerns. We believe, however, that when Hayley and Bill are visiting in their home, Paul and Gloria are within their rights to make their wishes known and provide separate sleeping arrangements.

What can parents do if their adult children choose to live together without the bonds of marriage? Realistically, very little. Pray and stay in the relationship.

AGING PARENTS

Eventually, your aging parents may become highly dependent. At what point do you take the initiative in helping them make decisions? What if they simply don't want your help and will not admit that they need it?

One survey participant wrote, "My dad lives in denial. He hasn't been able to drive a car for over a year but still talks all the time about getting a new van. Since my mom died, his health has failed and he won't be able to manage living alone much longer, but he refuses to talk about moving in with us or into an assisted-living community. He is also getting very forgetful but won't let me help him with his finances or other affairs. I'm an only child and don't know what to do."

When denial exists, it is harder to help an elderly parent. Perhaps our survey participant could consult with a social worker or his dad's doctor, CPA, or pastor. So how do you help parents who don't seem to want it? We've listed a few tips for you to consider:

- Consult with other family members and present a united front in offering help.
- Talk to your parent's pastor or other spiritual leader.
- Consult with agencies like the state or county office on aging.
- Talk to a counselor yourself for advice.
- Consult with your parents' doctor if you are concerned about their ability to function.
- In extreme cases, you may want to get legal advice.
- Find a support system for yourself. It may be a friend, relative, counselor, or clergy member with whom you can talk—someone who understands what you are going through and can bring objectivity to the situation.

FINANCIAL ISSUES

We remember Dave's mother once saying, "In my family, growing up we really didn't have lots money, so we just loved one another." Times have changed. Today's typical family has more financial resources than families years ago. Is it any wonder they also have more financial issues that cause misunderstandings and problems within the extended family? While in our survey only 6 percent of the participants said financial issues created the most stress, we believe financial issues often play into boundary issues, power struggles, in-law issues, communication, and various other potential sources of conflict.

Passing On Some Good Advice to the Older Generation

One great piece of advice we (Dave and Claudia) received when our children began to marry was to stay out of their finances. The world has changed in the years we have been married, and our families are living in very different times from when we were first married. Years ago we were not tempted by instant credit and credit cards. There were none!

I (Claudia) can remember when our paycheck ran out before the end of the month. We'd head for the North Georgia Mountains and spend a weekend with my parents. They graciously loved us, fed us, and let us use their washer and dryer—every load saved 25 cents! As we were leaving, they usually loaded us up with groceries and wonderful home-canned beans and applesauce. They never said that we were needy or made us feel guilty. They helped without getting involved in our finances.

While we have never lived near Dave's parents, I can't tell you the number of times Dave's mom, Lillian, was sensitive to our needs. Sometimes she slipped a crisp bill in a letter. It was never expected but always appreciated. By the way, she never asked about our finances, and by her example we learned to not feel responsible for how our married children handle their finances. And when we choose to help, we try to help in a way that doesn't foster dependency.

How your adult children spend their money is their concern, not yours. Before you become too critical, compare the world now to when you were first married. If we had had the option of credit cards and a line of credit at the bank, I'm not so sure we would have stayed out of debt. If you want to help, look for ways to help without producing guilt or indebtedness to you.

Helping with Strings Attached

We would assume that at some time or in some way all families face financial issues with loved ones. It's easy to use the purse strings to manipulate others in the family. Listen to this story: Susan and Jon come from very different backgrounds. Susan grew up in a modest home and completed college by working one semester and studying the next. She met Jon her senior year. His well-to-do parents footed all his college expenses and were quick to meet his financial needs. When Susan and Jon married, Jon's parents helped them get established in their first condo.

Their relationship with Jon's parents seemed okay, even though his parents were a little pushy and overbearing. Then they had the Big Conversation. It came after Jon and Susan had been married for two years. His parents were upset that they had not given them a grandchild. At this point, Jon's parents gave them an ultimatum—produce a male grandchild in five years or they would be disinherited. While extreme, this is a real story. Susan and Jon chose not to live under this constraint. Jon's parents cut off all financial help. The relationship also was cut off.

The Value of Money
A good deal of family stress revolves around money, even when manipulation is not a factor. The problem is not that we are all materialistic; rather, the money pit evolves because we all have different values. Some family members value a big house and others value a nice vacation. Some want nice cars, while others spend money on education. Some save for a rainy day; others give no thought for the future. Monetary issues can be at the center of the storm when we discuss extended family relationships.

Whatever you do monetarily with others, keep as your goal financial independence for all. Try to make financial goals mutual so that you are all working together. Recently, our (John and Margaret's) daughter wanted to go on an expensive school trip. Although we could pay for the whole thing, we decided the best policy was to split the cost with her. By so doing, we know that she literally made an investment of her time and money. If we had paid for the whole trip, we would have fostered a dependent attitude.

Helping Versus Enabling
There can be a real tension if you appear to be helpful to some family members and not to others. If you are in a position of being able to help needy family members, here's a good piece of advice: Don't play favorites! If you do, it can put a wedge in your relationships. At the same time you want to take the biblical admonition to help according to the need. And don't just think "financial." Maybe you will want to give an extra hand when a new baby arrives, or perhaps your parents need help making the big move from the family home into a condo or empty-nest house.

Tammy told us of the incredible family time she had with her seven siblings. They all met in California (sans spouses) to help their parents move from the home they had grown up in. She said it was like going down memory lane and that the time of working together to help her parents brought all the siblings into a closer relationship than they had been experiencing.

Also, watch out for feelings of entitlement. This relates to both sides of the generational seesaw. The older generation might feel, "I gave you the best years of my life—now it's your turn to pamper and take care of me!" while the younger generation might rationalize, "You have so many more resources than I do. Why can't you help me with a down payment on a house or help me buy the car that I really want?" One survey participant wrote, "The greatest tension in our extended family is that my younger brother thinks our parents should help to support his affluent lifestyle. I keep telling him that our parents really owe him nothing and that he should just grow up and learn to live within his means."

Should You Loan Money to Family Members?
You might remember the wise Polonius's advice to the youthful Laertes in Shakespeare's *Hamlet*. He says, "Neither a borrower nor a lender be." That is solid advice when it comes to relating to your extended family. Our first choice would be to give the money without expecting repayment—consider it a gift. However, if you do consider loaning money to an extended family member, we would suggesting doing it very, very carefully. It might be wise to draw up an official document and charge a modest interest rate. Also, talk about a repayment plan. What often happens with family loans is that the one who is borrowing the money is too optimistic about the ability to repay it. As time goes by, he or she feels guilty about

---

One survey participant wrote: "If I don't help my brother, I'm fearful of what he might do. He keeps borrowing money but never repays it. He's a little unstable and threatens to never speak to me again if I don't help him—so I usually cave in and loan him money." How would you respond to a financially manipulative relative? The tough love concept might be helpful. Just say no. Definitely don't loan him money that you need for something else. If you do loan him more money, realize that with his past record he won't repay you. Also realize that continuing to loan him money is making him dependent on you. You're not helping him solve his financial problems. Encourage him to get some counseling, and set up an appointment if he is willing to talk to a counselor.

not repaying the loan and starts to avoid the family member who lent the money.

Conversely, we think it is not wise to ask to borrow from family members, because it puts you and them in a precarious position. But if you do borrow from family members, you had better pay it all back on time. Otherwise, you may have hurt your extended-family relationship and it might take years to recover, if ever.

Develop Your Own Philosophy of Giving

What is your philosophy of giving? You might want to spend some time thinking about the following questions:

- Who in my family really needs help?
- If able, am I helping according to need?
- Do I tend to play favorites?
- Am I regularly giving to my church and missions or ministries I really believe in?
- Do I look beyond family for needs I can help meet?

RELIGIOUS AND CULTURAL DIFFERENCES

From our survey responses, one of the most daunting challenges deals with issues of faith. On one side are adult children who are praying that their parents will open their hearts to Christ. We (Dave and Claudia) identify. As we shared before, Dave's dad actually had a deathbed conversion. For this we rejoice, but during most of his life we knew him as a dear loved one who had zero interest in spiritual issues. How do you relate to a parent who belittles your faith in God and shows no interest in what is most important to you?

On the other hand, what about the concerns of parents whose adult children have made different choices? Perhaps they have joined a different denomination or their expression of Christianity is more liberal or more conservative than their parents'. Or perhaps they have converted to another religion or become totally secular. This brings up the issue of grandchildren who seem to be growing up without a strong Christian heritage. A grandmother wrote, "My daughter thinks I am too religiously conservative and has blocked all contact with my three grandchildren. I'm not even allowed to send my grandchildren Christmas or birthday presents. All I can do is pray. This situation hurts so much!"

The following story touches on many of the hard issues. We will actually share two versions of the same story: the parents' perspective and the son's. Again, our desire is to see the issues from both sides and foster more understanding and closer relationships, even though the parents and their son may never totally agree with one another.

The Story of Sam and Maneka

Sam, an American Christian, and Maneka, an Asian Hindu, met in graduate school and fell in love. Knowing a future together would present unique challenges, they were determined to surmount them together. Sam's parents were not so excited about the potential marriage:

> Our son, Sam, met Maneka in graduate school. The relationship went on for several years to the point that Sam and Maneka were thinking seriously about marriage. Because of the cultural and religious issues, we were concerned but said little, as we didn't want to harm the relationship with either Sam or Maneka. We realized that if we kept on bringing up our concerns in our conversations with Sam, we would be perceived as nagging, harping, and manipulative. Basically, we prayed and asked God for wisdom in how to relate to them. We knew at some point we needed to tell Sam how we felt and bring up our concerns.
>
> We began to pray for an opportunity to talk to our son alone. We also prepared what we wanted to say, realizing that each of us could say some things the other couldn't say—that Sam would receive some things better from Mom and some better from Dad. So first, we really prepared for the conversation. We also wanted to stick to the issues. We really liked Maneka as a person, but what concerned us were the religious and cultural differences that would also affect attitudes toward parenting.
>
> One day when Sam came over alone, it seemed like a good time to talk. We began by asking him about his relationship with Maneka. Then we said that we had some concerns but that we would only express them once—that we wouldn't bring them up again even if he

decided to marry Maneka. We affirmed our love for him and told him if he did choose to marry Maneka, we would be 100 percent support-ive—that we would receive her as our daughter-in-law and as the mother of our grandchildren, and that we would embrace her and welcome her into our family. Then, very cautiously, we shared our concerns with him. These were some of the issues as we saw them and what we shared:

Faith differences – "This is what we have observed. Loving one another is not enough. You need to familiarize yourself with her reli-gion. Hinduism is radically different from Christianity or Judaism or Islam." We gave him a book of world religions and suggested he read the chapter on Hinduism.

Culture differences – "There are major differences in how you take care of each other. How you celebrate Christmas, your religious tradi-tions. Our traditions mean much to us, and we want you to consider what you would be giving up in compromising and blending your two cultures. It may not seem important to you right now, but think about 10 years from now when you have children. It may be very important to you at that point."

Children – "Have you thought about your children all having Hindu names? That Maneka wants to move across the United States and maybe even to India—basically you would be divorcing your family and your background. She has her Ph.D. and plans to build a career that requires travel to India and around the world. She may not be there to nurture your children. She expects you to fulfill that duty of raising the kids. Are you willing to do this?"

We talked with our son as best we could without attacking him or Maneka. His response? He obviously was angry and irritated at us and accused us of being out of date, saying that just because his mom was a stay-at-home mom, that didn't mean it was the only way to parent children successfully.

We told Sam we weren't trying to tell him how to live his life, but as his parents we made our decision years ago, and we reminded him of how we had been there for him. Who would be there for his chil-dren? Who would get them to swimming lessons, Little League, band practice, and so on?

Well, we weren't sure we had done such a great job of talking to our son. When Sam left, he was not a happy camper. We loved our son and didn't know if our talk had helped or hurt.

A few weeks later Sam and Maneka called and wanted to talk to us. This conversation didn't go much better. It started with Sam saying that we didn't respect Maneka. We responded that we did respect her. She is really brilliant, beautiful, and charming, and we really liked her as a person. We continued:

"The more differences you have in a relationship—like education, heritage, religion, economic, cultural, age, and so on—the more challenges you will have to face in your marriage. More challenges increase the difficulty in building a marriage. You are both exceptional people, but you have lots of differences. When you add children, maybe it can be done, but it will take enormous work. We want both of you to succeed."

Let's stop the parents' story at this point and replay it from Sam's perspective:

I met Maneka, a beautiful young lady from Asia, in graduate school. Over the course of several months, we shared interests, developed a relationship, started dating, and fell in love. We dated for several years before we began to discuss the possibility of marriage. One night, I called my folks to tell them that Maneka and I were thinking about getting married.

This announcement was not a total surprise, but it presented an extreme crisis for my parents and for my relationship with them. A couple of weeks later, I went by my parents' home to pick up some stuff and became involved in a pretty spirited discussion. I could tell my parents had been preparing for the conversation, and in a way I felt trapped.

I assumed the biggest issue for them coming from a conservative background was that Maneka was not a Christian. They had grown fond of Maneka over the two years that they had known her from occasional visits and two beach vacations, and, of course, they loved me and wanted me to be happy, but they just did not feel that I should marry Maneka. A marriage between a Christian and a Hindu was not "right" in their way of thinking. But they also brought up other issues.

They thought I was being shortsighted—not thinking about life past graduate school. They also wondered if I was getting married for what they considered to be the wrong reasons—just because I was somewhat lonely and/or some of my other friends were getting married too. Concerning cultural issues, they had done their research, and I had to admit that the probability of divorce was higher under these circumstances. But Maneka and I knew we could make it work. They also brought up the issue of grandchildren that might come from the marriage who would probably not be raised in a Christian household. We have friends who have cross-cultural marriages and practice different religions, and their families are okay.

I reminded my parents that I was also a Christian, but that I had developed what I considered to be a more progressive outlook on life. Shouldn't they respect my brand of Christianity? Frankly, I did have some reservations about marrying outside of the Christian faith, but I loved Maneka and knew I wanted to spend the rest of my life with her.

Truthfully, I had not thought seriously about children—certainly not how to raise children. Nor did I have much real knowledge about how difficult it was to sustain a marriage that bridged two such difference cultures. But I loved Maneka, and we could overcome whatever obstacles life might present us with. But I certainly hoped I wouldn't have to choose between my parents and the woman that I loved.

This story told from two perspectives illuminates some of the most painful issues that our readers often have to face: generational differences ... cultural differences ... religious differences ... value differences. We left their story in midstream for a purpose. We realize we can't choose happy endings, nor do we always know what the results will be in 10, 15, or 20 years.

If Sam and Maneka marry, they will face complex challenges with no simple solutions. And for both sets of parents, having their child marry someone of another race, culture, and religion will understandably be difficult to accept—maybe even more difficult for Maneka's parents than for Sam's parents, who have already indicated they will indeed accept Maneka into their family. Saying it is one thing; living it out is another. Even if Sam's parents embrace Maneka, this marriage will still face more obstacles than one without such great cultural and religious differences.

The crisis that faces Sam and Maneka involves hard issues for these two families—as it would for most families. Some families that we know have a lot of multicultural and/or interfaith experience and might not perceive this potential marriage as the worst thing in the world, but for most families, the majority of the hard issues center on religion, generational differences, the sanctity of marriage (involving sexual activity and divorce), and grandchildren.

When we use the word *religion*, we don't just mean what brand, flavor, or denomination, but also what values and ethics are taught within a particular religious community. Frankly, we do not know any family that has not struggled with these kinds of issues. Perhaps we could say it in reverse: If you have not wrestled with one or all of these issues, then you are perhaps in some way missing out on the full extended family experience!

Jan Stoop and Betty Southard, in their book The Grandmother Book, emphasize the importance of prayer and suggest using Scripture in your prayer time:[4]

- Psalm 131—"O God, I do not concern myself about the things I place in Your hands. I keep my mind quiet and think on Your peace. I struggle to leave my concerns about _____ (insert person's name and/or specific concerns) there. But again and again I put my hope in You alone. Amen."

- The Lord's Prayer: Matthew 6:9-13—After reading or reciting the Lord's Prayer, write your own prayer to your heavenly Father—something like this: "Our Father in heaven, I honor Your name. I long for Your will to be done in me and in _____ (insert name) here on earth as it is in heaven. Meet my needs today for wisdom and strength. Help me to learn the way of forgiveness. Keep me on Your way. Lead _____ (insert name). Cover us with Your mighty wings, a shield against the Evil One. I acknowledge that all power and glory are Yours, forever and ever. Amen."

SUBSTANCE ABUSE

When a family member chooses to rebel and experiment with drugs, alcohol, and other negative behavior, everyone is affected. It's even more difficult if your family is well known. We (Dave and Claudia) sat across the table from Tullian Tchividjian, and over lunch he told us his story of how he wandered into the far country, and how his family helped to love him back home. Claudia had recently heard Tullian and his mother, Gigi Tchividjian, speak together at our church on the topic of "Prodigals," and we were eager to hear more of Tullian's story—especially as it related to the extended family and since his extended family is so well known. You may recognize his mother's name. Gigi Tchividjian, the mother of seven children, is a well-known Christian leader, speaker, and author of numerous books. She is also the oldest daughter of Billy and Ruth Graham.

Tullian came into this world with quite a heritage, and along with that came great expectations from the Christian community. He is even named after a respected Christian leader of the second century, Tertullian. Growing up in a large family, Tullian had three older siblings and three younger ones. Being in the middle, he often didn't know where he fit. "Sometimes I was linked with the older three and other times the younger three. But mostly, I felt alone.

"I don't know how I really slipped into such rebellion. I can remember beginning to use 'bad words' and misbehaving to get attention. One thing led to another, and I sank deeper and deeper into negative behavior. By age 16, I was so deep into drugs, drinking, and other really negative activities that my parents actually had the police come and remove me from my home. My parents were definitely justified in having me leave home, as I was disrupting the entire family. They had tried everything, but nothing seemed to help me. So in desperation they called the police to come escort me away from my home. For the next four or five years, I was in and out of jail and lived a really negative lifestyle."

We asked him if he felt a lot of pressure being Billy Graham's grandson and if that played into his rebellion. He replied, "Not really. Of course it would have been much more cool if Mick Jagger had been my grandfather, but I can't really blame my rebellion on the fact that my grandfather was so well known."

We were curious to hear what turned him back to God and to pursuing a healthy lifestyle once again. What could we learn that we could pass on to others to help them deal with their own extended-family rebels? Over the next two hours, Tullian shared with us some insights he had learned from his own experience. By the way, Tullian is now married with three adorable children and is a pastor on the staff of our home church, Cedar Springs Presbyterian Church, in Knoxville, Tennessee. Here's what he shared with us:

Stay in relationship. "My parents never wrote me out of the family tree. They continued to love me and keep contact as best they could. I can remember during those years, going home for holidays and seeing all my family and extended family. No one in my family cut me off, including my grandmother and grandfather." (If you know anything about the Graham family, you know they had to deal with their own rebels.)

We were especially interested in his grandparents' reaction to his rebellion and how they related to him during these years. "My grandmother was great. She would make light of things, like the way I dressed or the fact that I had pierced ears. She even gave me silly earrings. One Thanksgiving she gave me earrings that were a knife and fork. Another time she gave me Christmas tree decoration earrings. I always liked being around her. My grandparents always had a hug for me, and I knew that they loved me."

When talking to a family member about a hard issue, remember that you want to stay in relationship with this person, so choose your words carefully. You might want to review Challenges Two and Three for some tips on how to talk without attacking the other person. We suggest the following tips:

- Be prepared. Think ahead of time what you want to say. You may even want to practice.
- Talk to the other person alone.
- Have this conversation only once. Clearly express your concern and then leave it. Don't nag.
- Treat the other person fairly and with respect. No name calling.
- Don't use inflammatory words. Try to take the heat out of the issue.
- Be willing to hear the other person out.
- Pray, pray, pray.

"What advice did they give you?" we asked.

Tullian replied, "None. They didn't give me any advice or try to straighten me out. No lectures. But I remember my grandfather would tell me, 'Tullian, I know God's got His hand on you. I love you and I'm here for you. I know you're going through the valley right now, but I know my God and I know He'll take you through it.'"

Don't try to fix it. "I know it was really hard for my parents and family, but they didn't try to fix things for me. It must have been really difficult for them to keep a 'hands off' attitude, but they didn't want to enable me or become codependent. Also, they didn't threaten me or say, 'If you don't change, you are going to ruin your entire life,' or 'You need to get your life straightened out with God,' or 'How can you treat your parents like this?' I know it must have been so difficult for them to back off and let the Holy Spirit work—especially for my mom—but I'm so thankful that they didn't push or give up on me."

Tullian continued, "Along this line, I'd like to say that if you are dealing with a family rebel, you need to be really sensitive to the leading of the Holy Spirit. At times it may be appropriate to say something, but you need to make sure that your loved one has an open spirit. There is a verse in the Bible that says, 'Don't cast pearls before swine.' And that's what you do when you give advice to a person who is closed. He or she won't hear you, and you will drive the person further away. So if your loved one is hostile, give no advice—just love."

Pray, pray, pray. "Several times when the police came or called, my grandmother was visiting, and she would go to her room and pray for me. Prayer really makes a difference—I'm living proof of the miracle-working power of prayer!"

Love unconditionally. "I never questioned my family's love for me, and I know that was one thing that drew me back. Any way you can extend hope, encouragement, and unconditional love to your own rebel, do it. And never give up."

Practice patience. "Be as patient as you can be. Don't make mountains out of molehills, and give God time to work."

As we looked across the table over dessert, we were incredulous at what we had just heard and how indeed God had worked so mightily in Tullian's life. It gave us great encouragement for all those we know who are presently in the "far country" or traveling through a deep valley, and for their loved ones who so desperately want to see God work in their lives.

May Tullian's story encourage you. Just a few months before our lunch together, we attended Tullian's ordination at our church. As he was officially becoming a pastor, his grandfather was conducting a crusade in Cincinnati. If you watched the broadcast, you may remember him saying how proud he was of his grandson on that evening; how his grandson who had been through the darkest valley was now, as he spoke, being ordained a minister. God does indeed work miracles.

LEARNING TO COPE

In the last few pages, we have looked at several of the really hard issues extended families face. Not all of them are solvable. Many are perpetual issues that will be around for a long time. How can we learn to cope with them? Some situations are truly tragic, like the following. A woman in our survey wrote about her abusive childhood, her mentally ill mother, a dying middle-age sister, and her own chronic medical problems. Her husband's family faced an equal number of hard issues. Still, this woman tried for years to pull the extended family together and support them, but she ultimately realized the futility of the situation. She received absolutely nothing in return. Sadly she wrote to us, "Now, I am very ill and it's like I have no family. It's disappointing to me to put in all that work, I guess, in vain."

Frankly, we don't believe that all of her work was in vain—although we are sure that it seemed that way to her at the time. Perhaps she was not storing up treasure on earth, but she certainly will receive a reward in heaven—where neither moth nor rust nor extended family can consume! She perhaps planted seeds that must be watered and cultivated for years before growth happens and fruit is found. We hope she doesn't totally give up on her efforts. We do believe, however, that this woman needs to honestly evaluate the situation, give up her dream of the perfect family, and make the best out of the rest.

Even though we would all like a trouble-free family, all families struggle and all families have their own difficulties to accept and overcome. The issues vary, of course, from family to family. Issues that are hard for one family to deal with might be simple for another, and the reverse may be true as well. Unfortunately, some families have had to cope with divorce on numerous occasions and may know how to better relate to each other than a family who has never experienced a divorce. Similarly, some families are enriched by religious and cultural differences, while other families are destroyed by them. We have discovered no consistent, predictable pattern here. So what can we do?

Realize You're Not Alone—Everyone Struggles

When our (John and Margaret's) children were young and they had experienced a bad day, the inevitable selection for bedtime reading was *Alexander and the Terrible, Horrible, No Good, Very Bad Day*. This is a simple tale of a young boy who has a terrible day. Nothing goes right at school, at home, or with his friends and family. Our children somehow felt better at night knowing that Alexander—though fictional—knew what it was like to have a bad day.

Know that you are not alone in your struggles with your family. Many saints throughout history have struggled through this life, and you are even now surrounded by "a great cloud of witnesses" (Hebrews 12:1). And guess what? They had difficulty with their extended families too! If you don't believe us, just read about the families in the Old Testament. They say that misery loves company, but we say that misery needs company when the going gets tough. We all need support from people who have experienced our problems.

On a deeper level, regarding complex problems, the painful truth is that little can actually be done—at least in the short term. Therefore, it is important for you to accept the fact that none of us has control over every matter under heaven. Theologically speaking, this means that we must learn to admit that we are not God, and that we are all finite, limited, and sinful creatures who fall short of His glory.

Practice the Power of Prayer

Second, pray. Prayer helps a lot. Prayer is the best medicine that we know. Prayer even has an effect on the one who prays, and prayer also has an impact on our God—the author of every good and perfect gift and the creator of extended families.

Years ago, Reinhold Niebuhr penned a helpful prayer that has become popularly known as "The Serenity Prayer" and has been used by millions of folks who are in desperate circumstances. Read these words prayerfully and adopt them as your own: *God, grant me the serenity to accept the things I cannot change, courage to change the things I can, and wisdom to know the difference.*

Praying this particular prayer (or a similar one) seems to have an impact on us: It soothes our souls and presses us to do only those things which matter or help. But also do not be afraid to pray for specific things, understanding that ultimately we should want God's will to be done. Here, Jesus is our model. You might recall that He earnestly prayed in the Garden of Gethsemane to avoid the time of trial, but concluded His prayer by surrendering His will, saying, "Yet not my will, but yours be done" (Luke 22:42). Do not be afraid to ask God for exactly what you want.

Both the Arps and the Bells will testify personally to the power of prayer in our own lives. But remember that ultimately our goal should not be to exert our own will but to see that God's will is done—and we are not God! God's ways are higher, more mysterious, and more marvelous than our ways. So pray for your loved ones and trust them to His loving care, and do what you can to maintain a relationship with them, which is the next part of our coping strategy.

Stay in Relationship

We suggest that you do what you can to stay connected and in relationship with those who are mired in difficulty or with those making life difficult for everyone. All too often when people are angry or disappointed with others, they shut off communication as a means of self-preservation, but ceasing communication only makes things worse in the long run. Far better (and more effective) is to continue to remain in contact until an opportunity for reconciliation occurs. Yes, it may test your patience and your faith. You may need to "turn the other cheek" and "go the extra mile," as Jesus encouraged His disciples to do. But who knows when the light of God might shine down upon all parties and a new day might dawn? Nothing is impossible with God.

By staying in relationship, you might find yourself in a better position to be a positive witness and influence on others. Look again at the story of Jesus with the Samaritan woman at the well (see John 4). A Samaritan woman with a shady past went to Jacob's well at noon to draw water. She was an unlikely candidate to engage in a discussion of matters of faith with Him. Nevertheless, Jesus initiated a conversation with her. By simply speaking with her and by developing a relationship with her, Jesus changed the life of this woman forever! She was most impressed that Jesus knew everything that she had ever done—all the many bad things! Yet He talked to her kindly and with great grace. One theologian, the late Paul Tillich, even suggested that acceptance of others (not finger pointing, blaming, judging, or condemning) actually creates repentance. His claim is consistent with our experience and, we believe, consistent with the grace that God shows rogue characters in the Bible.

Lovingly Share Your Perspective

Do not be afraid to state your opinions and to set your own boundaries, but do so lovingly. Admittedly, this is tricky business! When Gloria and Paul were confronted with the sticky issue of Hayley and Bill sleeping together, we think they should have stayed true to their convictions and told Hayley and Bill that they did not think they should sleep together until they were married. If Hayley and Bill felt differently, then Gloria and Paul should have exhibited the courage of their convictions and have been prepared for an appropriate defense. We don't expect everybody in an extended family to agree on morals, but neither do we believe that anything is gained by keeping things secret. Families are best served when hard issues become part of the public discourse—as long as truth is declared in love!

Taking the Log Out

Remember, Jesus tells us to get the log out of our own eye before we remove the speck from the eye of our neighbor (Matthew 7:3-5). This, of course, is great advice. Sometimes it is easy to see how others tear up the family with their behavior, but most of us have a certain blindness to our own behavior.

The Book of Proverbs reminds us that we all do what is right in our own eyes. We suggest that you take a good, hard look in the mirror and try to find ways that you can facilitate positive family relationships before you find fault with relatives. If others know that you are working on your relationship with the family, then perhaps they will be inspired by your example to do the same.

Deal with your own inappropriate actions and reactions by following the following steps:

- Step one: Write down what is irritating you about the other person or the situation.
- Step two: List your own inappropriate actions or reactions.

• Step three: Write down how you wish you had responded.

• Step four: Ask the family member for forgiveness for your own part.

Life is too short to waste a lot of emotional energy on things that probably will never be resolved. Far better to enjoy the blessings that God gives you than to continually covet those things that you do not have. We are reminded of the story about the man who sold his farm and went all around the world looking for riches and died penniless in the process. What he failed to discover was that the backyard of the farm he sold was covered with acres of diamonds![5] If he had stayed home and enjoyed what he had been given, he would have been a rich man.

The story is a parable about life: We would be far richer if we spent our days cultivating what we have been given by God instead of embarking on some fruitless quest. Applying that lesson to our extended family, life is really too short to chase some extended-family dream that is just that—a dream— or concentrate on what is negative. Try to enjoy what you have while you have it. Concentrate on the positives of your extended family. It may help to realize that some extended families are just closer than others. Remember Challenge One, where we talked about how important it is to have realistic expectations for our family.

A Prayer for Contentment

Teach me how to find contentment as I grow older.

Teach me how to be a person others want to be around, not avoid.

Teach me how to enjoy the gift of life,
    to enjoy each day, to have no self-pity.

Teach me how to treasure memories
    and plan for tomorrow with enthusiasm.

May I be thankful for the times we as a family
    go our separate ways.

May I be thankful for the special times
    we feel like a family again.

May I be thankful for the privilege of being family.

—WRITTEN BY JANE BELL (JOHN'S MOTHER) IN 1993

Also remember that life is long. Problems that appear painful at present may not be considered painful in the long sweep of life. When we look back on some of the hard issues that we have had with our own extended families, most of them have simply faded away. Time cures a lot of problems and heals a lot of wounds. Let time work for you. One of the things we often ask ourselves in dealing with hard issues is, "Will this matter in five years? Ten years? In the light of eternity?" This means, obviously, that patience is one of the great keys to dealing with hard issues.

Keep Hope Alive

Finally, never give up hope. In the Christian faith, despair is considered a sin because Christians have been given a great hope in Jesus Christ. The prophet Isaiah proclaims that one day we shall experience what some have called a "peaceable kingdom." The wolf shall live with the lamb, the leopard shall lie down with the kid, and the calf and the lion and the fatling shall be together (see Isaiah 11). Let us cling to Isaiah's promise that one day somewhere, at some time, peace shall reign. We encourage you to be realistic, but do not lose hope for your extended family. God is full of wonderful surprises.

Understanding Boundaries and Extending Beyond Family

Standing in the checkout line at the grocery store, the man behind me mumbled, "Only one more meal and she goes home!" I (Claudia) smiled, and that seemed to encourage him to continue. "My mother-in-law has been here for the whole week—seven long days—and tomorrow she goes home."

"Don't you get along with her?" I asked.

"No, we see eye-to-eye on very little. She just doesn't like the way I or my wife and kids do things. For instance, I cook all the meals for her and try to please her, but all she does is complain about how I prepare the food. I'm Italian and she hates Italian food. I only have one meal to go, and then she leaves. I can't wait!"

"I'm just curious. I'm a mother-in-law, and I'd be interested in what advice you would give to your own mother-in-law if you thought she would take it."

"Advice?" he said. "I'd tell her our lives are just different from hers and she needs to accept us and our lifestyle. I really do try to adapt and please her, but she is totally inflexible, plus she crosses all of our boundaries. Orders our kids around and is critical of my wife, her only daughter. If she would just stay out of my kitchen we'd get along better, but no, she's there criticizing me and telling me what I'm doing wrong."

As I loaded my groceries in the trunk of my car and headed home to the Arp family gang—everyone had holed up at our house for the Thanksgiving holidays—I wondered what my own daughters-in-law would say to a stranger in a grocery store in a similar conversation. How would they evaluate me? Would they say I respected their boundaries? Do they respect mine? When we visit them do they ever think, "One more meal and they go home"? I certainly hope not! But this chance conversation with a stranger gave me cause to consider the importance of setting and respecting boundaries within our own extended family.

Perhaps you're familiar with the Robert Frost quote, "Good fences make good neighbors." Do good fences (or boundaries) make for good extended-family relationships? We believe they do. And if we're right, how do we establish and respect boundaries within our extended family? We would suggest two steps. One, evaluate present boundaries and, if needed, make a midcourse adjustment. Two, look for ways to extend your life beyond family.

SETTING AND RESPECTING BOUNDARIES

Robin and Jackson know firsthand why it's important to set boundaries. They learned the hard way. When they first married, Jackson set no boundaries with his mother, and it spelled disaster for his marriage. Family boundaries are biblical. In Genesis 2:24 we read, "For this reason [marriage] a man will leave his father and mother and be united to his wife, and they will become one flesh." That's setting new boundaries where your spouse comes before your parents. Jackson finally learned why it was so important to leave his mother and cleave to Robin. Here's their story of how he finally came to set healthy boundaries. By doing this, they restored their own relationship and laid the groundwork for healthy extended family relationships as well.

"From the beginning of our marriage," Jackson said, "our biggest issue was not my mother-in-law; instead, it was Robin's mother-in-law. Yes, my mom."

Robin agreed wholeheartedly. "Jackson's mom just had a way of getting in the middle of our lives, right between us. She visited us frequently, and most of her visits were unannounced. She freely interjected her opinion in our conversations and always seemed to disagree with me. If I said the walls were off-white, she would say, 'No, they're yellow.' And where was her only son, Jackson, my husband, in this conversation? Being the peacemaker, he would say, 'Actually, the walls are a yellowish off-white.' I was furious; he never took my side or defended me."

The result? Robin became so dissatisfied that after two years of marriage she moved out for several months.

"I couldn't believe Robin left me! But slowly," Jackson said, "I began to analyze what had happened here, and I realized I was really at fault. Robin was my wife. *She* was the one I had chosen to spend the rest of my life with, not my mother—and my unwillingness to set some boundaries with my mom had driven Robin away. How had I been so blind? I just thought Mom was being Mom, and I had never taken Robin's complaints seriously. Now she was gone, and that was very serious!

"To repair our relationship, first I needed to have a heart-to-heart talk with my mom. I asked Robin to go with me and to hear what I had to say to Mom. Robin was incredulous but very pleased. Here is what I told Mom:

"'Mom, I have asked Robin to move back home, and I have made the following commitment to her concerning my relationship to her and to you. Please listen closely to what I have to say. I am totally committed to Robin; she is the one I chose to marry, and I will never ever leave her. I am committed to her for life. She is my wife, and she will always come first in my life. I love you and I always will, but I will not let you come between Robin and me. In the future I will always choose to support Robin, even if I feel she is wrong. Please make no attempts to divide us. This is just how it is going to be. I'm sorry that I have not supported her in the past.'"

Did establishing boundaries through this conversation make a difference? Absolutely! Did Jackson's mother test his new resolve? Absolutely, but he held firm. It was several months before his mother began to accept this new reality. It also took time for Jackson to reestablish trust with Robin. As Robin began to realize that Jackson was serious, her relationship with her mother-in-law became much more positive. Actually, the relationship between Robin and her mother-in-law improved drastically. And when Jackson's mom was critically ill in the hospital, it was Robin who stayed with her and helped nurse her back to health. Today they have a great relationship.

Russell and Sophie are another couple who have struggled with boundaries. When they married, Russell didn't realize the impact Sophie's close-knit Italian family would have on their marriage. After eight years of marriage, Sophie is still really close to her parents and talks to her mom four or five times each week. Russell has come to accept that Sophie's family is more involved in their lives than is his family, but over the years they had to work at finding the right balance and establishing boundaries. When we asked Russell about his in-laws his response was, "Well, they are extremely hands on! I wouldn't want to spend two weeks together, but three days is okay. Actually, we get along fine now, but at first we had some really rough spots."

He related one crisis time that was a turning point in his relationship with Sophie's parents—especially her dad. "I was in graduate school and we had been visiting our parents, who both lived in the same town. Sophie and I had a horrendous argument. I can't even remember what we were arguing about, but we knew we needed to resolve the issue before we got in the car and started our eight-hour drive home. When we stopped by to tell my mom good-bye, we walked in the house and told Mom we were having a disagreement and needed to work things out before we left and that we were going to the back porch to talk. During our heated discussion, Sophie's mom called to say good-bye again, and Sophie told her we were having an argument. She didn't know that her mom would turn around and call her dad. The next thing I knew, her dad left work, came to my parents' home, and walked straight through to the back porch and angrily confronted me: 'Why is my daughter upset? What have you done to her?'

"Somewhere I got the courage to tell him, 'Your daughter is my wife, and it's none of your business what we are arguing about or even if we are arguing. I love her dearly, and together we are going to work things out without your interfering.'

"It took a while, but slowly a light went on for Sophie's dad. He began to realize that his daughter was married, that he had even symbolically 'given her away' during our wedding ceremony, that our allegiance was to each other, and that when we had a disagreement it was up to us to work things out. That was several years ago, and he has never crossed that boundary again."

Because Russell was willing to be firm with his father-in-law, he and

Sophie have a better marriage and a better relationship with their extended family. They are all better equipped to face the many challenges and curve balls that life presents to them.

The principle of setting boundaries and making your partner and your nuclear family number one is a solid, biblical principle that will improve extended-family relationships. But what about the situation when generations must live together in the same house?

When Generations Live Together Under One Roof

Jennifer's elderly mother-in-law lived with her for two years. Jennifer still had two teenagers at home, and her husband's mother was all too quick to tell her grandchildren what to do.

"The most difficult part," Jennifer told us, "was when Curtis's mom would contradict what we had already told our sons. It was really confusing for them. Her failing health was the reason we had her move in with us, and since Curtis traveled a lot in his work, I was the one who took care of her on a daily basis. Sometimes Curtis would ask me to go on a short trip with him and I'd reply, 'I'd love to, but someone needs to be here to care for your mother.'

"This got very old, since his mom also crossed my boundaries. I would

---

Ways to Make Living with In-Laws Work

- Keep your sense of humor, and be flexible.
- Talk and listen to each other. Have planned times of communication. You may decide to have a family management meeting on Monday evenings and resolve any issues.
- Set reasonable house rules, like "You get it out, you put it back. You mess up the kitchen, you clean the kitchen."
- Write down guidelines and financial arrangements so there are no misunderstandings about what was agreed upon.
- Respect each other's privacy.
- Together talk about what each person needs most to make this work. ("I need a living room without clutter." "I need real coffee in the morning." "I need a time to relax and play the piano." "I need space.")

go into my bedroom to grab a few moments alone and regroup, and within five or ten minutes she would be calling for me or knocking on my bedroom door. Usually what she wanted could have waited for a few more minutes.

"One time when Curtis asked me to take a short trip with him, I agreed to try to work it out. We hired someone to come into our home and stay with his mom. She wasn't happy about it, but she got along just fine. I was just sorry I didn't do this sooner. I also began to have someone come in for a couple of afternoons each week so I could have some privacy and time of my own. Setting this simple boundary made a huge difference in my relationship with Curtis's mom and my attitude toward caring for her.

"After two years, the small house next to ours became available and we moved Curtis's mom into her own little home. Then we hired someone to come in daily to be with her. That has worked so much better, and we enjoy our frequent times together. My relationship with Curtis has less tension, and we're all relating to each other much better. Our sons even enjoy visiting with their grandmother, and she seems to be respecting our boundaries much better."

When the Nest Refills or Never Empties
Sometimes when the nest empties, it soon begins to refill with adult children, in-laws, and maybe even grandchildren. On the other hand, for some the

---

If as an adult child you are moving back in with your parents, it is vitally important to keep several issues in mind.

- First, it is a privilege—not a right—to be invited and/or welcomed home as an adult.
- Second, your parents' lives do not revolve around yours, and any demands that your moving back home put on your parents' routine should be discussed and dealt with.
- Third, financial issues, job issues, dating issues, school issues, children issues, and lifestyle issues are your issues. If—and only if—your parents agree to share your issues do they become theirs as well.
- Fourth, never assume anything—ask, clarify, and clarify some more so that true communication may occur.

family nest never empties, and adult children continue to live at home with their parents.

In a poll of 1,000 college students conducted by jobtrack.com, 61 percent said they planned to live with their parents after graduation.[1] While for many this is temporary, of unmarried American men between the ages of 25 and 34, more than one third are still living at home.[2]

For the first year of my (Claudia's) parents' marriage, they lived with my grandmother. In-law relationships are hard to maintain in a normal setting, and they can be extra stressful when you must temporarily live together. However, there are situations today when you may need to make room in your nest. When this happens, how can you make the best of it? You can start by asking yourself what you can do to make this time harmonious and pleasant. Also, determine to be flexible.

When adult children come home to roost with parents and sometimes bring a spouse and even grandchildren, it's easy for them to slip back into the child role. While we have never personally experienced living with parents or having our younger families live with us, we asked others who have for suggestions. The best advice we've gotten is to "talk, talk, talk!" and to "listen, listen, listen!"

You can handle stress better when you realize "this is temporary" and when at least one other person understands how you feel. If you have a supportive mate, great. If not, find a friend who will be willing to listen and to encourage you. Some bicycles are built for two, but few houses are adequate for two adult generations. However, our friend Janet tells us it can be a positive growing experience. Janet does suggest having a game plan, setting specific guidelines.

Together work out guidelines for financial arrangements, household chores, even rules for pets. (Yes, some bring a menagerie of animals.) If there are grandchildren, include baby-sitting arrangements. You may want to renegotiate each month and set a time of evaluation to ask, "How is this working?"

Then, remind yourself why you are doing this. It may be a way to help your offspring temporarily. If it's permanent, do what you can to give each family privacy and breathing space. Don't be a doormat or a dictator. Balance *is* there. Find it—your future relationship depends on it!

Meeting Basic Needs

In setting boundaries with extended family, it may be helpful to understand that each generation, from children to the elderly, has similar needs, and that when these needs are met, boundaries tend to be respected. We all need food and shelter. But we also need to love and be loved—to know that others really care about us. We need affection, respect, tenderness, acceptance, dignity, honesty, trust, and hope. And as much as possible, we need freedom from pain. Which of these needs we can provide for our loved ones depends on our present relationship with them and our own life circumstances. By taking steps to meet the needs of our extended family, we may reduce many of the relationship problems we have been looking at.

Pushing the Positives

When boundaries are crossed or disrespected, try to be the more mature person and react positively. Sometimes the offending person can feel so isolated and alone that when you show interest and affection, the relationship will improve dramatically. So whether you are blessed with relatives who are positive and are in good health, or whether you are in a more distressing situation with relatives who are negative and perhaps in poor health, look for ways to express interest and build positive bridges.

Frances's father called several times each day and continually asked her to take him to the drugstore or grocery store or hardware store. Frances knew he

---

Financial Guidelines for Living at Home

We believe the more clearly things are spelled out before your son or daughter moves back home, the better. If he or she is working and has any means of paying rent, we think it's a good idea. Adults pay for housing; why shouldn't your adult child? It will help you both maintain more of an adult relationship. We suggest the following guidelines:

• Rent should be agreed on by both parties before he or she moves in.
• Write a simple contract or agreement so there will be no confusion as to the amount of rent, when it is due (day of the month), and the length of the contract (for instance, three or six months).
• The month before the contract ends, renegotiate it and also discuss if this is the time for your son or daughter to now move out.
• Let him or her know you see this as a short-term arrangement.

was lonely since her mother's death and tried to accommodate him as much as possible. But after several months she became weary. So she began to look for opportunities to get him around other people. For instance, she picked him up each Wednesday night to go with her to the church dinner. As she gave him more attention, he began to be less demanding. Once she surprised him with an impromptu shopping trip and bought him a new shirt. Her dad was thrilled. He loved looking through all the stores and being with his daughter for the whole afternoon. Assured of her love and attention, he began to call less frequently, make fewer demands, and respect Frances's boundaries a little better.

Look for something you know your relative would like to do and then surprise them. While you can push the positives, you need to realize that you can only do what you can do. You simply can't be all things to all people, so refuse to give in to false guilt. You should not feel responsible for what you cannot control, and with extended family relationships, little is under your direct control. If you're facing a really hard situation, we encourage you to get advice from others.

A great extended family verse is 1 Peter 5:7: "Cast all your anxiety on him because he cares for you." Also, in Psalm 56:3-4 we read: "When I am afraid, I will trust in you. In God, whose word I praise, in God I trust; I will not be afraid."

We believe the validity of our faith in God is lived out in our relationships. Certainly, family relationships are some of the most challenging ones in which to live out our faith. As we conducted our survey on extended family we asked people, "Do you know one extended family where there are no strained relationships?" The answer was usually no. Stress is part of living together as families, but we can handle that stress better if we put our trust in the Lord to care for our loved ones and help us relate to each in a positive way.

When you're struggling with boundaries or with negative relatives, it's easy to also become negative. So to change your focus, make a list of their positive traits. Then express them. You might want to write a letter, send an e-mail, or make a phone call just to say something positive to that family member you are struggling with.

What Are Your Boundaries?

Boundaries relate to all extended family relationships, not just to marriage, parents, or adult children. You might want to think for a moment about your own extended family. What are the present boundaries, spoken or unspoken? Do the grandparents and parents in your family understand and respect each other's boundaries? What are the boundaries for grandparents in relating to grandchildren? Should they get involved in giving directions to or correcting grandchildren? Of course, situations vary. A casual visit from grandparents who live several states away would be different from the grandmother who provides daily after-school care for her six- and eight-year-old granddaughters.

Respect Parenting Boundaries

It's hard enough to be a parent; it's even harder if there's extended family watching and waiting for you to mess up. One young mom shared her frustration. Her mother-in-law kept her three-year-old son for the weekend. When she picked him up, her mother-in-law had washed *and* ironed all of his clothes, including underwear and T-shirts, and she had written out detailed instructions for how to wash her grandson's clothes, including details such as "turn clothes inside out before placing in the washing machine." This mom wanted to turn her mother-in-law inside out!

Ways to Be a Supportive Grandparent

- Spend time with your grandchildren without their parents around.
- Plan one-on-one times with each grandchild.
- Listen to your grandchildren—they are fascinating people!
- Enrich their lives with your experiences and talents. If you play a musical instrument, give music lessons if they are interested.
- Go to their activities such as plays, piano recitals, and soccer games.
- Make pizza together.
- Choose before grandchildren arrive what you want to be called. Otherwise, one of the first nonsense syllables uttered in your presence may become your name.
- Don't iron underwear!

One grandmother in our survey indicated that she spends most of her time worrying about her grandson. She disapproves of how her daughter-in-law is choosing to raise him and just knows he will end up being a juvenile delinquent. Another grandmother worries about a granddaughter who is in her thirties.

What about baby-sitting? A good friend who has five grandchildren has charted her own course. Her advice is, "Keep kids if it is convenient and if you want to do so. But remember, being a martyr will not build your relationship with your grandchildren or your daughter- or son-in-law."

Some boundaries are imposed by circumstances. Boundaries for relatives who live in the same geographical location and see each other often will be different from those who live far away. So you will need to evaluate your own situation. Now ask yourself, do you need to set boundaries or respect the boundaries of others?

EXTENDING BEYOND FAMILY

Our last challenge to you to is to extend your life beyond family. In other words, "Get a life of your own!" You will be much more interesting to the rest of your kin if you resist centering your life only on family. Sadly, some parents struggle with releasing their children into adulthood. Letting go may be hard, but the rewards of letting go and reconnecting on a more mature adult level are worth the effort.

Allison told us, "I'm 25 years old, and my complaint is that my parents have become so needy and insecure since I left home. I know they love me and want me to love them, but their constant attention is just driving me away. I want parents who are confident and self-assured; parents who respect my boundaries and have a life of their own. It's too big of a responsibility to be the center of their world."

Allison's parents need to extend their lives beyond their daughter. It's a huge burden to feel responsible for your parents' happiness—one that Allison doesn't want to have. It's also an unfair burden for an adult child, who has enough struggles coping with the new responsibilities of adulthood. Some parents find it difficult to let go and release their children into adulthood because they have fallen into the trap of basing their sense of self-worth on their children.

Security and Significance

Stop for a moment and consider what is your source of security and significance. If you're looking to your children, grandchildren, or extended family for purpose and meaning in life, you're looking in the wrong place. We believe that it is only possible to find real security and significance in our relationship with God. And when we find our purpose and meaning in life in Him, we can let go and love our family in healthy ways.

Another reason for moving on and extending our life beyond family is that when we are really involved in life, we will be less likely to compete with the nuclear family. In our world today, sometimes we idolize family—and especially the Norman Rockwell picture of the happy and delightful extended family. If there were problems within your family growing up, those problems are whisked away with Norman's paintbrush, and happiness is restored. Many unrealistically assume the extended family can be closer than their own nuclear family was during the growing-up years.

As we have said before, we believe the extended family will never be— nor should it be—as close as the nuclear family. When we realize that the nuclear family should and always will come first, we can move on to develop healthy extended-family relationships.

So how can we find the right balance of loving our extended family without smothering them?

Get a Life of Your Own

Did you hear the story about the elderly couple who in their nineties got a divorce? When asked why they waited so long, they replied, "We were waiting for all our children to die."

Believe it or not, some parents are so tied to their children they refuse to get a life of their own. This attitude doesn't make for great intergenerational relationships. The younger generation doesn't need parents hovering overhead like a helicopter, nor do they want to feel responsible for their parents' personal happiness. So don't allow yourself to be too dependent on your married children and their spouses. It's not good for you or for them! Look for ways to build your own supportive friendships and to grow as a person. Enjoy the fact that your active parenting years are over.

If you represent the younger generation, don't foster too much dependency on your parents. Keep as your first priority your spouse and children.

Your parents should realize you don't love them less, but they can't be the focal point of your life. Encourage your parents to continue to grow and develop new interests.

When Beth and Hal's children were grown and married, they moved to another part of the country. For the first couple of years, it was an adventure. They remodeled their 1930s home and enjoyed having time to get back into tennis and boating. But eventually they missed the kids, so they decided to beef up their friendship circle. They started inviting others over for dinner.

Together they planned the menus and grocery shopped. Since they were both still working, they found shortcuts such as prepared sauces for their gourmet entrees. They discovered they actually enjoyed entertaining, and a whole new world opened up for them. They still miss their adult children and are thrilled when they visit, but at other times they have their own life and their own friends.

If your life is lonely, let us encourage you to look outward. We all share difficult circumstances. Everyone has problems of one sort or another. The choice is yours—to concentrate on your problems or to expand your world. Perhaps now is the time to "get a life."

While you value your past, think now about how you can improve your future. Begin by taking a personal inventory. What relationships do you

---

You are never too old or too young to start something you would like to do. Consider the following:

- Take an art class (or calligraphy or ceramics, etc.).
- Try a writing project—poetry, fiction, journal.
- Take up digital photography.
- Learn a new sport.
- Expand your knowledge of the Internet.
- Learn to play the piano, clarinet, flute, or other instrument.
- Take voice lessons.
- Take a gourmet cooking class.
- Get involved in volunteer work.
- Become a mentor for a young person.

enjoy? Is there something you used to do that you enjoyed? Whatever you did before, you may be able to do it better now. We know one lady who, at 69 years old, bought a piano at a garage sale. Six years later she bought a baby grand piano, and now, in her late eighties, she still practices two hours a day. She even plays for weddings and other special events.

Reach Out to Others

In Romans 12:13 we read, "Share with God's people who are in need. Practice hospitality." And Hebrews 13:2 tells us, "Do not forget to entertain strangers, for by doing so some people have entertained angels without knowing it." It is our belief that healthy families learn how to incorporate others by reaching out and expanding their circle of family into the community.

We (John and Margaret) recall the early days of our marriage when we lived in a different state from any of our family, and our vacation time and budget were seriously limited due to the demands of seminary. Our favorite SEC football team made it into one of the big New Year's Day bowl games, and we had no family to watch and celebrate with. So we planned a party and started inviting all the people we knew in town with connections to or interest in the bowl game who didn't already have plans for the holiday.

We looked up some of our childhood friends who were living in the city and invited them to come and bring their spouse or a date. Then we started preparing to feed the expected crowd—five pounds of shrimp, roast beef sandwiches, three kinds of dip, fruit platter, cheese platter, desserts, and beverages. Then the calls started coming—Jeff and Lisa couldn't come because she was on call; Mary and Joe couldn't come because they got last-minute tickets to the game; Angela and Jim couldn't come because his parents

---

When my (Claudia's) mother at age 90 was dying, her home was filled with visitors coming by to see her one last time. Many who came were young families with young children. I asked her, "Mother, how do you know all these young families?" To which she replied, "Years ago, my mother gave me some good advice. She said 'Catherine, when you lose a friend make two younger friends.' I've practiced that all my life!"

decided to come visit for the holiday weekend. So we figured out who we knew at the seminary that had any ties to our hometown, and we extended the invitation to them. Some already had plans and some could come, and we still had room—so we invited some of our neighbors, figuring that if their car was there they didn't have plans and they might like football.

Well, what a motley crew we were. It would have been easy to whine and complain about not being able to be with family or even really close friends, but we had a wonderful time and discovered the incredible thing that happens when "strangers" and "hospitality" are combined—new friendships are formed, connections are made, and pretty soon it feels like family.

Forming Your Own Social Network

For the five years we (Dave and Claudia) lived in Vienna, we created our own social network among Austrians, Americans, and international families. Without extended family close by, we adopted other families as aunts, uncles, and cousins and built some new traditions.

Each year we had a Super Bowl party and introduced our Austrian friends to American football. Once we also had a *Sound of Music* party. Our Austrian friends were amused at the American slant on the Von Trapp family.

If you live away from your extended family, we encourage you to look around and adopt some family. Your own family life will be enriched.

Be Family for Singles

A family in one of our former churches adopted a widow who had no family in town. Every Sunday they sat with her in church and included her in their extended-family holiday meals. What a beautiful example of extending hospitality beyond family. This family is living out 1 Peter 4:9: "Offer hospitality to one another without grumbling."

My (Margaret's) mother has often told me of my own grandmother's Sunday tradition. My grandmother was a teacher and a church organist most of her life, and my mother is an only child. Every Sunday my grandmother would cook a huge pot roast with all the trimmings, and my mother would ask, "Who is coming to lunch today?" My grandmother would reply, "I don't know for sure. Whoever needs to come."

She would then look for people at church who she thought could use an invitation to her family Sunday dinner. She would find students visiting from the university or a widow or widower without family in town, or a young couple on a strict budget, and fill her dining room table with strangers. My mother got to meet some of the most interesting people and hear the most amazing stories every week. She also saw the gift of hospitality in action.

Find or Be Surrogate Grandparents

Quite a few years ago when our (John and Margaret's) girls were little, an elderly couple who had never had children of their own decided that they would claim Megan and Katie as their surrogate grandchildren. Every holiday they would mail a greeting card with a sweet note and a crisp dollar bill to each of the girls, and at church they would be sure to seek them out to say hello and give them a hug. Their kindness and generosity was rewarded with the genuine gratitude and affection of two young "grandchildren."

Share Family Holidays with Others

Another family has a huge extended family in town with aunts, uncles, cousins, brothers, sisters, mothers, fathers, children, and a wonderful matriarch. Every Easter this family gathers at the grandparents' place in the country after church for a family Easter picnic with canoeing, horseshoes, an Easter egg hunt, and a delicious barbecue. The matriarch of the clan has a little gift for everyone present.

However, part of her tradition is to include those who don't have family in town to celebrate with and who have to be in town because of their job—like the preacher and the organist/choirmaster and the associate and youth ministers—the church worker orphans. One time when she was commended for her generous hospitality she said, "I really am doing this for a selfish reason. When we have guests, everybody is on their best behavior and tries to really get along."

Build Your Own Marriage

We (Dave and Claudia) were speaking to a group of parents who were entering the empty-nest stage of family life and one big concern surfaced. "What do we do now that our children are grown?" asked one mom. "We just don't know each other anymore." Many who experience the empty nest have little in common with their spouse. Sometimes it's as if their marriage relationship had hibernated until their children grew up and married. Their children had been the focus of their family life, and the temptation now was to be overinvolved in the lives of their adult children.

When your own marriage is dull or less than satisfying, it's easy to become emotionally dependent on your adult children and their spouses. If you are single at this stage of life, it's time to build positive relationships with other adults. For all, it's time to broaden your horizons to include people other than your offspring. And if you are married, let us encourage you to focus on your marriage.

Even if you still have children at home, you can begin planning for how you want to enrich your marriage when the nest empties. For years we talked about taking a trip to New England the autumn after all our sons had left home, and it actually happened. The trip allowed us to set fresh goals for our marriage and enjoy being just two again.

A word to the wise: Don't wait until your children grow up to build your marriage. Now is the time to build for the future. Look at the time you have right now and use it. Your married children will benefit from a parental model of a healthy love relationship.

Serve Others

We believe that family is extremely important or else we would not have devoted so much of our own lives to helping other families. And within your families, we believe you should take great care to work together, celebrate life, and let that elusive "domestic tranquility" reign. We also believe you should protect and nurture your family, but at the same time understand that family

---

Ways to Build Your Own Marriage

- Start dating your mate. Plan a date with your mate for this week.
- Plan a 24-hour getaway for two.
- Read a book on marriage. Two we recommend: The Second Half of Marriage and 10 Great Dates to Energize Your Marriage.
- Sit down with your spouse over a cup of coffee or tea and talk about your hopes and dreams. Don't talk about your kids and in-laws.
- Take a marriage course or attend a marriage seminar.

is not an end in itself. We cannot make an idol out of our family. Jesus challenged His followers by saying, "If you love those who love you, what reward will you get? Are not even the tax collectors doing that? And if you greet only your brothers, what are you doing more than others?" (Matthew 5:46-47). Properly, the family should be thought of as an earthen vessel through which we can love and serve our neighbors and our God.

Stretching out to embrace and include others is exceedingly healthy and, we believe, absolutely necessary. Sociologists tell us the best test of the strength or health of a nuclear household is how easily or how well an outsider can be included at the dinner table or other family gathering. We have always had great respect for those families who organize and serve a meal for singles and lonely people on Christmas or Thanksgiving Day, or who take time on special holidays to volunteer at a homeless shelter.

Service also can happen in the ordinary times of life. I (Margaret) was amazed to hear that a friend of mine picks up four children from school every day. What makes this amazing is that two of the children are hers and two are from other families. When I asked her why she was doing this she replied, "Well, Meg's parents are divorced and her parents both work, and she would go home to an empty house every day because she is too old for day care and too young to really be by herself—so she just comes to my house. Lea's mom is a single mom who worries about Lea, and it is just as easy for her to come to my house too." We realize that this is a serious form of responsible hospitality being modeled for all of us, and we are challenged to care for others from this mom's example.

What can you do to reach out and serve others? We (Dave and Claudia) have a passion to help strengthen marriages, and we spend much of our time leading seminars and writing books to help couples improve their marital relationship. Actually, our work in marriage education has a boomerang effect on our own marriage and extended-family relationships. We feel we are better parents, grandparents, and in-laws because we are actively involved in working on our own marriage and helping others. Once we asked one of our sons what he wanted for his birthday, and jokingly he replied, "Two weeks of your life." We laughed, but deep down we felt good that our son saw our lives at this stage to be so appealing.

Our involvement in our work in marriage education keeps us from being too doting, possessive, and overinvolved in the lives of our extended family.

One fringe benefit of our frequent travel is that we often get to visit family on the way home from a speaking event.

We (John and Margaret) feel fortunate that our girls are in a school and church environment that actively encourages—even expects—community service to others on a regular basis. It is most often during a visit to a homeless shelter, or a trip to an equine therapy ranch for kids with special needs, or on the way to or from a hospital or nursing home visit, that we are privileged to see and hear firsthand how much our children want to make a difference in someone else's life, and how much they take to heart the Bible verse, "From everyone who has been given much, much will be demanded" (Luke 12:48). They understand through their experience that it is in the service of others that true meaning and purpose is found.

Expanding the Family Circle

Do you know the difference between the Dead Sea and the Sea of Galilee? They are connected by the Jordan River; however, there is a major difference between these two bodies of water. As you would assume, the Dead Sea in southern Palestine is dead! Almost nothing grows in or around it. On the contrary, the Sea of Galilee to the north is green, lush, and full of life. What makes this difference? The major difference is that water flows into *and out of* the Sea of Galilee but only *into* the Dead Sea. In the same way, if a family cares only for itself—if nothing is flowing out—then it will be tough for its members to grow and develop. On the other hand, if love (and everything else that makes for a happy home) flows into, through, and out of family to others, life flourishes.

Another great picture is the Jewish celebration of Passover. On Passover, our Jewish friends leave a chair empty and the door to the house ajar. This is because they are expected to be ready for Elijah to return. Likewise, we think that our families should always be prepared to include the surprise guest at the table whenever an old family friend might appear. In the Last Judgment scene in the Gospel of Matthew (25:31-46), the King says that when you feed, clothe, nurse, visit, or provide drink to "the least" of those in your midst, you have done so to Him! We hope and pray that you will extend your family to include the least of those in your midst.

We see family as expanding circles. The smallest circle in the center is the core family—mom, dad, and children. The next circle includes grandparents, in-laws, aunts, uncles, and cousins. This is the circle on which we have concentrated within the pages of this book, but it is only the beginning of the many ways family can make a difference in our world.

The next circle draws in our church family and includes those who are lonely, single, or have family far away. Other close relationships in the church may become "adopted" aunts and uncles and grandparents. In many ways, the church can offer loving support for families through activities like parenting and marriage programs and small fellowship groups.

When the church family is alive and growing, its influence extends into the community—our next expanding circle—and offers support to families in the various neighborhoods by sponsoring community outreach programs. The ever-expanding family circle also includes our nation and our world. We can make a difference in our world, one family at a time.

Being Family

What are your expectations now as you think about being family? Are they more realistic than when you started this book? Have you been encouraged to go beyond chitchat and to really speak the truth in love? Are you challenged to work at being more civil, calm, and clear when you don't see eye-to-eye with your own extended family members?

We hope we've given you some helpful suggestions for harmonizing the times you get together as an extended family as well as motivated you to build better relationships with the whole family clan. And what about those hard issues we all face? Hopefully we've helped you to develop your own coping strategy and helped to strengthen your determination to stay in relationship and love unconditionally.

As you consider your own boundaries and how you can reach out to others, we want to encourage you to consider one last question. What are you doing to leave a legacy for your nuclear and extended families and for others in your church, community, nation, and world? The challenge is before us. Together we can make a difference.

Notes

Chapter 2

1. *New York Times 2002 Almanac*, ed. John W. Wright (New York: Penguin), p. 287.
2. Ibid., pp. 287-89.

Chapter 3

1. Evelyn Bence, *Leaving Home: The Making of an Independent Woman* (Philadelphia: Bridgebooks Westminster Press, 1982), p. 84.

Chapter 4

1. Nigel Rees, *Cassell's Humorous Quotations* (London: Cassell & Co., 2001), p. 93.
2. Flannery O'Connor, *A Good Man Is Hard to Find* (New York: Harcourt, Brace, Jovanovich, Inc., 1953).

Chapter 5

1. Rodney Clapp, *Families at the Crossroads* (Downers Grove, Ill.: InterVarsity, 1993), pp. 86-87.
2. Adapted from Pier Forni, *Choosing Civility: The Twenty-Five Rules of Considerate Conduct*, as excerpted in *Parade Magazine* (August 25, 2002), p. 8.
3. Adapted from Dianne Hales, "Why Are We So Angry?" *Parade Magazine* (September 2002), pp. 10-11.
4. Harriet Lerner, *The Dance of Anger* (New York: Harper & Row, 1985), p. 4.
5. Ibid., pp. 123-24.
6. Adapted from David & Claudia Arp, *Love Life for Parents* (Grand Rapids: Zondervan, 1998), p. 50.

Chapter 6

1. Jennifer Crichton, *Family Reunions* (New York: Workman Publishing, 1998), p. 4.
2. We have found the following resources to be helpful in planning family reunions: Thomas Ninkovich, *Family Reunion Handbook: A Complete Guide to Planning and Enjoying Family Reunions* (San Francisco: Reunion Research); and Jennifer Crichton, *Family Reunion: Everything You Need to Know to Plan Unforgettable Get-Togethers* (New York: Workman Publishing).

Chapter 7

1. Gail Sheehy, "It's About Pure Love," *Parade Magazine* (May 12, 2002), pp. 6-7.
2. Adapted from David and Claudia Arp, *The Second Half of Marriage* (Grand Rapids: Zondervan, 1996), pp. 157ff.

Chapter 8

1. A helpful resource for those who have experienced infidelity or are on the brink of divorce and want to restore their marriage is the Retrouvaille program. Web site: www.retrouvaille.org.
2. Barbara LeBey, *Family Estrangements* (Marietta, Ga.: Longstreet Press, 2001), p. 134.
3. Focus on the Family can be reached by phone at 800-232-6459. Mailing address: Focus on the Family, Colorado Springs, CO 80995. Web site: www.family.org.
4. Jan Stoop and Betty Southard, *The Grandmother Book* (Nashville: Thomas Nelson, 1993), pp. 253-59.
5. Russell H. Conwell, *Acres of Diamonds* (New York: Berkley Publishing Group, 1986).

Chapter 9

1. "Now Here's a Scary Statistic," *New Choices Magazine* (November 2000).
2. Gail Sheehy, *New Passages* (New York: Random House, 1995), p. 49.

About the Authors

Claudia Arp and David Arp, MSW, are founders and directors of Marriage Alive International, a ground-breaking ministry providing resources and training to empower churches to help build better marriages and families. The Arps are popular conference speakers, columnists, and authors of numerous books and video curricula, including *10 Great Dates to Energize Your Marriage, Love Life for Parents, Empty Nesting,* and the Gold Medallion Award-winning *The Second Half of Marriage.*

Their Marriage Alive seminar is esteemed both in the United States and in Europe. Frequent contributors to print and broadcast media, the Arps have appeared as empty nest experts on the NBC "Today Show," CBS "This Morning," and Focus on the Family. Their work has been featured in publications such as *USA Today, The Christian Science Monitor, Reader's Digest, Marriage Partnership,* and *Focus on the Family* magazine.

David and Claudia have been married for 40 years, have 3 married sons and 8 grandchildren, and live in Knoxville, Tennessee.

Contact Marriage Alive at www.marriagealive.com or (888) 690-6667.

FOCUS ON THE FAMILY®

$\mathcal{W}$elcome to the $\mathcal{F}$amily!

Whether you received this book as a gift, borrowed it, or purchased
it yourself, we're glad you read it. It's just one of the many helpful,
insightful, and encouraging resources produced by Focus on the Family.

In fact, that's what Focus on the Family is all about—providing
inspiration, information, and biblically based advice to people in
all stages of life.

It began in 1977 with the vision of one man, Dr. James Dobson, a
licensed psychologist and author of 18 best-selling books on marriage,
parenting, and family. Alarmed by the societal, political, and
economic pressures that were threatening the existence of the American
family, Dr. Dobson founded Focus on the Family with one employee
and a once-a-week radio broadcast aired on only 36 stations.

Now an international organization, the ministry is dedicated to
preserving Judeo-Christian values and strengthening and encouraging
families through the life-changing message of Jesus Christ. Focus
ministries reach families worldwide through 10 separate radio
broadcasts, 2 television news features, 13 publications, 18 Web
sites, and a steady series of books and award-winning films and
videos for people of all ages and interests.

•   •   •

For more information about the ministry, or if we can be of help to your
family, simply write to Focus on the Family, Colorado Springs, CO 80995
or call 1-800-A-FAMILY (1-800-232-6459). Friends in Canada may write
Focus on the Family, P.O. Box 9800, Stn. Terminal, Vancouver, B.C. V6B 4G3 or
call 1-800-661-9800. Visit our Web site—www.family.org—to learn more about
Focus on the Family or to find out if there is an associate office in your country.

We'd love to hear from you!

More Family-Strengthening Resources
From Focus on the Family®!

Peacemaking for Families
Whether it's sibling rivalry or marital spats, family conflict is a fact of life. But with the valuable principles and engaging real-life stories in *Peacemaking for Families*, you'll learn how to create a harmonious environment based on basic conflict resolution skills found in Scripture. Bless your family with peacemaking skills!

Don't just get by...FEAST ON LIFE!
Maintain a vibrant faith, grow marital intimacy, guide your children to success, and achieve peace, harmony, and victory in every aspect of your life—just as God intended. Overflowing with biblical teaching, practical examples, step-by-step instructions, and real encouragement, *Soul Food and Living Water* offers the spiritual nourishment needed to overcome the challenges faced by today's African Americans.

Make Anger Your Ally
Do you ever struggle with anger? You can suppress it, deny it, let it control you, or you can *Make Anger Your Ally*. Popular author and clinical psychologist Neil Clark Warren will show you how to make anger work for you rather than against you—how to master anger and transform its energy into a dynamic force for positive living.

The Gift of Grandparenting
When your children have children, it's a whole new world of love and joy. And as parents get busier, grandparents are increasingly important influences in the lives of their grandchildren. Whether your grandchildren live around the corner or around the world, *The Gift of Grandparenting* will give you new ways to enjoy your special role and to bless your grandchildren.

• • •

Look for these special books in your local Christian bookstore—or you may request them from us. Either log on to family.org or call Focus on the Family toll-free at 1-800-A-FAMILY (1-800-232-6459). Friends in Canada can call 1-800-661-9800. You may also send your request to Focus on the Family, Colorado Springs, CO 80995. In Canada, write Focus on the Family, P.O. Box 9800, Stn. Terminal, Vancouver, B.C. V6B 4G3.